CW00432423

'This book will have a major role in fusing the often false dich
The case studies are written reflectively and will stimulate u:
at our practice. There is variety here, and a number of ger
relevance to professionals in all sectors. The book has been e
from experienced professionals who are highly respected in ᴛʜᴇ ʜᴇʟᴅ ᴏʟ ᴄʀᴅ. ʟᴛ ᴇʟʟᴇᴄᴛɪᴠᴇʟʏ uses a
wealth of evidence drawn from practice.

It will be immensely valuable for teachers, school leaders and others who have an involvement in
professional development in education and illustrates well how CPD can provide the basis for all
students to receive the best and most effective learning opportunities.'

Professor Ken Jones, Editor, *Professional Development in Education* Journal

'This book is a really useful tool that colleagues who are at different stages of developing their
professional learning offer can use for themselves, the teams they work in and the organisations
they are part of. It helps them to celebrate all the hard work that is currently happening in the
area of professional learning for the whole school workforce or as a stimulus to help probe
personal thinking about how Headteachers/CPD leaders can move professional learning forward
in their own school or organisation.

The case studies provide a range of diverse topics that are relevant to schools and educational
institutions in the current and changing landscape of education. They are clear, concisely written
and helpful. It was exciting (as well as exhausting) to read about all the work that is going on at
the moment and I feel really proud to be part of such an impressive learning community.'

Rebekah Iiyambo, Headteacher, Kaizen Primary School

'As a teacher in a PRU I was especially delighted to see that Peter Earley and Vivienne Porritt have
included a chapter in their book for the Special School setting entitled "Coaching in
the special school: making teachers and support staff feel more valued". So many times we
can be overlooked.

Contributions from practitioners with a wealth of experience have made this book either re-
affirming, motivating or thought-provoking for any CPD leader. Through the use of case studies,
the reader is taken through the journeys of primary, secondary and special needs schools and
how the impact of the changed practice of their CPD has helped to raise standards and staff
morale. The final chapter considers the TDA's new Professional Development strategy for the
children's workforce in schools, 2009–12, launched in the summer of 2009.

Whatever school setting you may be teaching in, or whatever stage of CPD development you
have reached, you will find this book a valuable resource.'

**Tessa Brown, CPD Leader, Tunmarsh Pupil Referral Unit (PRU),
London Borough of Newham**

Effective Practices in Continuing Professional Development

.

Effective Practices in Continuing Professional Development
Lessons from schools

Edited by Peter Earley and Vivienne Porritt

First published in 2009 by the Institute of Education, University of London,
20 Bedford Way, London WC1H 0AL
www.ioe.ac.uk/publications

© Institute of Education, University of London 2010

British Library Cataloguing in Publication Data:
A catalogue record for this publication is available from the British Library

ISBN 978 0 85473 883 0

Design by Hobbs the Printers Ltd, Totton, Hampshire SO40 3WX
Printed by Elanders

Contents

Acknowledgements

We would like to thank the Training and Development Agency for Schools (TDA), especially Tom Leftwich and Liz Francis, all organisations involved in the *Effective Practices in CPD* project and, in particular, the schools involved in the case studies, for enabling the London Centre for Leadership in Learning (LCLL) to contribute to, support and research the key area of professional development.

Foreword

Effective professional development is a key driver for school improvement. These aren't empty words – this important book, and the case studies it contains, makes this abundantly clear.

The pivotal word is, of course, *effective*. Professional development has been part of school life for many decades, but sometimes it has been seen as something 'done to' staff rather than as a right and a responsibility, and it hasn't always been linked to whole school improvement and better outcomes for children and young people.

As this book illustrates so well, this is changing. Schools are becoming far more aware of the transformative power of continuing professional development (CPD) and of the need to develop their own capacity and capability as part of a self-improving, self-sustaining system. A highly skilled and motivated workforce needs to be part of this.

The focus on the team around the child requires a different approach to CPD. As noted above, CPD is a right and a responsibility. The Professional Standards for teachers now require staff to 'evaluate their performance and be committed to improving their practice through appropriate professional development' and post-threshold teachers are expected to contribute to the development of others. The National Occupational Standards (NOS) are comparable standards for school support staff. They also set out expectations for staff development.

Schools have never been short of highly skilled *individuals*, but these individuals have not always worked as collaborative partners in whole-school teams. The case studies in this book illustrate that in our most successful schools all staff – both teachers and support staff – work closely together to achieve shared goals in a culture that values adult learning, with a strong focus on the impact this has on improved outcomes for children and young people. They also illustrate that organisational, team and individual development must go hand in hand.

So what is *effective* CPD?

It's a question this book goes a long way towards answering. At the TDA our core aim is to provide the information, programmes and resources that schools, CPD leaders and school staff require. What better way to ensure we do this than to develop them collaboratively with schools – by asking schools and their staff what they need and by carrying out research?

The research was conducted by the London Centre for Leadership in Learning (LCLL) at the Institute of Education, University of London. It has been a pleasure to work with such a professional organisation and the 600 schools and other organisations that contributed to the project.

The project's findings support and extend existing data from a range of other studies (many supported by the TDA). They show clearly that a combination of a number of core factors makes CPD *effective*.

First, professional development must involve and include the whole workforce – that is, school leaders, teachers and support staff. Sometimes this may mean that all staff engage in the same training and development; more frequently, it means tailoring development to groups or individuals.

Strong leadership is also vital – not only from headteachers (although their support is critical), but also from CPD leaders and other senior staff. As this book illustrates, this is most effective when CPD leaders champion professional development and work with colleagues to design and deliver a variety of CPD programmes that meet the needs of schools and individuals.

Schools must have a learning culture where colleagues talk about learning and teaching more than anything else. To make this work, schools need to have a clear and shared vision of what effective development looks like at the outset of their CPD. They need to ask themselves: 'What difference will it make?' at the start of each development activity, not at the end.

Professional development needs to build on staff experience and, through continuous enquiry and problem-solving, enable them to develop additional knowledge and new teaching and learning strategies. This is most effective when it is collaborative and supported by the coaching and mentoring of more experienced colleagues.

Evaluation is also critical. It's impossible to know if professional development is effective – and how to make it even more effective – unless you can accurately ascertain its impact on teaching and learning and pupil outcomes.

The 2006 Ofsted report *The Logical Chain* identified that much of CPD in schools is not evaluated in terms of its long-term impact on individuals' professional practice. To ensure learning gained through CPD is effective and sustainable, it is vital that effective impact evaluation is developed. And what better way to do this than by asking children and young people? This is why the TDA's impact evaluation tool places young people at the heart of evaluation (see http://www.tda.gov.uk/upload/resources/pdf/i/impact_evaluation.pdf).

Perhaps most important of all, it is essential that CPD is an entitlement and a responsibility for all staff. Embedding a learning culture in which CPD is a core part of school processes, linked to high-quality performance management and whole-school improvement, means it becomes part of a coherent cycle. *Effective* CPD practice is strategic and sustainable.

To fully achieve this, school leaders need to build explicit and cyclical links between improvement planning, CPD, performance management and the national standards that set out what's expected in a role.

More and more schools are making these links (as shown by the case studies in this book), with very positive results. At the TDA we're committed to helping these schools sustain and extend this work and to support other schools to develop connections. Our three professional development priorities – to embed a learning culture, to increase coherence and collaboration, and to improve quality and capacity – are being taken forward through our work with clusters of schools and support for CPD leaders.

With the help of schools, we've developed an extensive national database of CPD programmes and resources to help you wherever you are on this journey. The database, which is currently in its pilot stage, helps you to explore a wide range of CPD opportunities, compare information from a variety of providers, and confidently choose what's right for you and your school.

We are now planning, with the help of the LCLL, to develop resources to help schools explore the effective practice set out in this book. This will complement our existing and extensive online CPD guidance and resources. In addition, we are going to make it possible for the schools involved in the research to share their individually developed CPD practice and resources through our new CPD database.

Finally, I would like to thank all the colleagues who have worked with us, showing how practice and policy are best developed together.

For more information about the TDA's CPD support, including Professional Standards, National Occupational Standards, case studies illustrating effective practice, resources and other practical guidance, visit www.tda.gov.uk/cpd

Liz Francis
Director of Workforce Strategy
Training and Development Agency for Schools

Notes on contributors

Sara Bubb has an international reputation in staff development and new teacher induction. As well as being a senior lecturer at the Institute, she is England's Advanced Skills Teacher network leader and was the *TES* new teacher expert. She is directing the DCSF research project on outward-facing schools, led the TDA staff development outcomes study, the *From Self Evaluation to School Improvement* project and helped evaluate NCSL's *Future Leaders* programme. Her many books include *Successful Induction, The Insider's Guide for New Teachers* and, with Peter Earley, *Helping Staff Develop in Schools* and *Leading and Managing Continuing Professional Development.*

Peter Earley is a Professor of Educational Leadership and Management at the London Centre for Leadership in Learning at the Institute of Education, University of London. His central research interest is leadership and professional development and he has recently completed studies of accelerated leadership development programmes and an evaluation of the National Professional Qualification for Headship pilot programme. He has published widely in the field of school leadership, school evaluation and professional development and his books include: *Leading and Managing Continuing Professional Development* (second edition, 2007) and *Helping Staff Develop in Schools* (2010), (both with Sara Bubb and published by Sage). Peter was co-director of the TDA's *Effective Practices in CPD* project.

Liz Francis taught in London schools for five years prior to working for 14 years in a number of government agencies including the QCA where she worked on public examinations and 14–19 policy. Liz left QCA to work for Suffolk LA as a senior adviser during which time she also worked as an Ofsted inspector. Her key responsibilities in Suffolk were the secondary national strategy, 14–19 education, specialist schools and commercial services to schools. She left Suffolk to work at the Training and Development Agency for Schools where she is currently Director of Workforce Strategy.

Steve Illingworth is a Secondary Strategy Teaching and Learning Consultant for a Local Authority in the North West of England. For most of the period covered in this study he was Acting Secondary Strategy Manager for the LA. In both of these roles, he has supported several of the borough's secondary schools with the development of their coaching programmes. He has co-written three History textbooks in the Folens 'Specials!' series (1995-6) and, more recently, has had two articles published in the *Times Educational Supplement*.

Steve Lloyd has over 30 years of experience in schools and higher education (HE) in the UK. This included being a deputy headteacher and acting head in two secondary schools. Whilst in HE he led a number of collaborative learning development projects, including facilitating the introduction of the South West's first Innovation Lab, iSpace. He has also worked on several contracts overseas developing Global Education and Leadership Development at organisational, system and senior levels. He is currently Director of the Networked Learning Partnership Ltd, an educational consultancy organisation focusing on designing and delivering collaborative approaches to system-wide change.

Margaret Mulholland is an educational consultant with 15 years' experience in Initial Teacher Education and Continuing Professional Development. Her work is primarily involved in developing, supporting and linking effective practices across London schools, leveraging her extended connections with London school leadership. She developed the Secondary Employment Based Routes at the Institute of Education and worked with Professor Tim Brighouse and subsequently the Specialist Schools and Academies Trust to establish the London Challenge Programme of Leadership Visits. Coaching and Mentoring is a further area of expertise and development with the LCLL and most recently with the Education Advisory Boards in Northern Ireland.

Vivienne Porritt is Executive Director for the London Centre for Leadership in Learning, Institute of Education, University of London. She sees the continuing professional development of all colleagues as central to achieving improvement, working with schools, local authorities and national agencies to support a coherent approach to CPD. Key aspects include the strategic leadership of CPD and performance management and an innovative approach to impact evaluation. Vivienne's background is secondary headship. She also works as a consultant to the DCSF for Chartered London Teacher status and for the TDA, on the national Leadership of CPD project. Vivienne was Director of the *Effective Practices in CPD* project.

John Tandy worked as a regional CPD Adviser for the DfES and subsequently the TDA, raising awareness of effective CPD practices and developing partnerships in the North West. He began his career as a teacher of foreign languages and moved on to senior school leadership. He now works as a consultant with a Local Authority on school workforce issues, working with CPD leaders and teachers in the early years of their career as well as the wider school workforce. He also works with Teachers TV as a CPD Adviser supporting the use of Teachers TV as a CPD resource.

Carol Taylor is CPD Project Leader at the London Centre for Leadership in Learning at the Institute of Education, University of London. She is currently working with CPD leaders and has been involved in the national TDA project looking at effective professional development practices. She is module leader of the 'Innovative Leadership of CPD' on the IOE MA Leadership programme. She has also written and leads on the professional learning programme of the graduate training programme at Hertfordshire University. Her background is school senior leadership teams and a particular focus of her current work is developing an innovative and inclusive approach to performance management and impact evaluation.

Abbreviations

AfL   Assessment for learning
ALS   Action learning set
AST   Advanced skills teacher
BME   Black and minority ethnic
CPD   Continuing professional development
ECM   Every Child Matters
ECT   Early career teacher
EPD   Early professional development
EPPI   Evidence for Policy and Practice Information and Co-ordinating Centre
EYFS   Early Years Foundation Stage
GTC   General Teaching Council
GTP   Graduate Teacher Programme
HEI   Higher education institution
HLTA   Higher level teaching assistant
ITT   Initial teacher training
LA   Local authority
LCLL   London Centre for Leadership in Learning
LSA   Learning support assistant
MLE   Managed Learning Environment
NCSL   National College for School Leadership (now known as National College
         for Leaders of Schools and Children's Services or the National College)
NPQH   National Professional Qualification for Headship
NQT   Newly qualified teacher
Ofsted   Office for Standards in Education, Children's Services and Skills
PM   Performance management
PSHE   Personal, social and health education
RQT   Recently qualified teacher
SEAL   Social and emotional aspects of learning
SEF   Self-evaluation form
SEN   Special educational needs
SENCO   Special education needs coordinator
SLT   Senior leadership team
TA   Teaching assistant

TDA   Training and Development Agency for Schools
TLA   Teacher Learning Academy
TLR   Teaching and learning responsibilities

Part 1

Effective Practices in Continuing Professional Development project

Chapter 1

Introduction

Peter Earley and Vivienne Porritt

- CPD matters
- *The Effective Practices in CPD* project
- Impact evaluation
- Main findings
- The structure of the book

In this introductory chapter we attempt to set the scene and briefly describe the nature of professional development and its importance, thus outlining the context in which the Training and Development Agency for Schools (TDA) funded the *Effective Practices in Continuing Professional Development* (CPD) project and how it was set up. After this short discussion of the importance of developing the school workforce, we briefly describe the project. An approach to impact evaluation developed at the London Centre for Leadership in Learning (LCLL) was used to provide the foundation for the LCLL support given to the school-based project leaders. We will outline the main features of this approach to impact evaluation in this chapter. This is followed by a brief discussion of the main findings of the project; and the factors and approaches that make for effective CPD. These findings are further considered in the final chapter and in the light of the detailed case studies presented in Part 2. Finally, we will outline the book's overall structure.

CPD matters

Continuing professional learning and development are central to the success of any school or college. People are the prime resource of any organisation and better results (whether defined in terms of productivity, parental or customer satisfaction, profitability, employee retention, examination scores or other performance indicators) are more likely to be achieved by managing and developing people better. As long ago as 1972, the James Report stressed that each school should regard the continued training of its teachers – we would now say 'school workforce' – as an essential part of its task. This government report ensured that the further professional development of school staff became a national issue and, as stated by the TDA's Liz Francis in the Foreword, it still is today – for the simple reason that people development is crucial for the improvement and growth of institutions. The workforce is the most important resource of any organisation, but especially in people-based institutions like schools, colleges and other educational settings. The TDA's strategy, which we discuss further in the final chapter, is important in ensuring that workforce development continues to be high on everyone's agenda.

As the bulk of educational organisations' budgets are devoted to wages and salaries, it is crucially important to maximise colleagues' contribution to improving children and young people's learning and well-being. The professional learning and development of the workforce is a key component for developing students' learning. Ongoing people development is key when identifying organisational priorities to bring about improvement and enhance the quality of teaching and learning. In *The Logical Chain* Ofsted found that 'schools which had designed their CPD effectively and integrated it with their improvement plans found that teaching and learning improved and standards rose' (2006, p.2). Overall, professional learning was found to be most effective in those schools where the senior staff had a clear understanding of the connections between each link in the chain, were aware of CPD's potential for raising standards and therefore gave it a central role in planning for improvement.

But what exactly do we mean by CPD? The TDA define it as follows:

> *Continuing professional development consists of reflective activity designed to improve an individual's attributes, knowledge, understanding and skills. It supports individual needs and improves professional practice.*
>
> (TDA, 2008, and www.tda.gov.uk/cpd)

Another, more detailed, definition states that CPD is:

> *an on-going process encompassing all formal and informal learning experiences that enable all staff in schools, individually and with others, to think about what they are doing, enhance their knowledge and skills and improve ways of working so that pupil learning and well-being is enhanced as a result. It should achieve a balance between individual, group, school and national needs; encourage a commitment to professional and personal growth; and increase resilience, self-confidence, job satisfaction and enthusiasm for working with children and colleagues.*
>
> (Bubb and Earley, 2007, p.4)

Or, put more simply, CPD is about the learning and development of the school workforce, ultimately for the purpose of enhancing the quality of education for the school's children and young people. Clearly, CPD matters: it is crucially important for school and college leaders to give it high priority and to lead and manage it effectively. The main aim of the TDA's *Effective Practices in CPD* project was to help schools improve their provision and evaluation of CPD for the school workforce. It also aimed to help the TDA increase its understanding of the nature of effective CPD. We next turn to a brief consideration of the project.

The Effective Practices in Continuing Professional Development project

The *Effective Practices in Continuing Professional Development* project was made up of two phases: in phase one, which ran from the autumn of 2007 to the autumn of 2008, the TDA awarded grants of up to £20k to 232 school-based CPD projects in England. As well as local authorities and higher education institutions, over 670 schools were involved in the project. Of the 232 projects involved in the first phase, just over two-thirds (68 per cent) submitted successful proposals for phase 2 and were awarded grants of up to £10k. The second phase of the project ran from the autumn of 2008 to the end of March 2009.

All of the CPD projects were related to one or more of seven key focus areas:

- professional and occupational standards
- Science, Technology, Engineering and Mathematics (STEM) subjects
- 14–19 provision
- schools facing challenging circumstances
- extended schools services
- early professional development (EPD)
- impact evaluation.

The grants were awarded in November 2007 and the LCLL was given the task of monitoring the projects, providing support with project management, reporting and impact evaluation, and identifying emerging issues. In early 2008, the TDA hosted four regional conferences for participating projects and delegates were given the opportunity to discuss the successes and challenges of their projects, explore the LCLL's framework for impact evaluation, receive input and support from LCLL, and meet and network with representatives of other projects in their region. The programme itself was structured around self-review by project leaders, with LCLL project and regional consultants supporting and monitoring progress. Project leaders were required to produce reports of their project's progress and in regular meetings with the TDA we offered our professional judgement of the emerging practices as reported by project leaders and LCLL regional consultants.

Most of the projects had 'CPD impact evaluation' as their main focus. 'Early professional development' (EPD) and 'Professional and occupational standards' were also popular areas. Fewest projects were found in the '14–19 provision' focus area. However, within the seven focus areas, the central concerns of the projects were often wide ranging and the case studies that follow in Part 2 give examples of the various areas covered. We did not find the focus areas to be an important variable regarding effective CPD; other factors were more significant regardless of the project's focus area.

The projects were often led by headteachers (24 per cent), especially in the primary sector, deputy heads (15 per cent) and assistant heads (14 per cent). One-third of projects worked with higher education institutions and two-thirds with external consultants and trainers. About one in seven institutions involved all of their staff in the project; one in five involved at least 50 per cent of staff; and about one-quarter of projects involved 25 per cent or less of the whole staff. Approximately seven out of 10 projects involved support staff in their project, the most common being teaching assistants (and other pupil support roles) followed by administrative staff. About one-third of project leaders reported having had some black or minority ethnic staff (BME) involvement in their projects. Also, the vast majority of projects (94 per cent) were linked to the school or college improvement plan.

For some projects, as will be shown in the case studies in Part 2, the experience was very significant and many teachers and other staff felt motivated and valued as a result. The projects helped improve their practice and reiterate much of what was said earlier about the importance of CPD in schools. They led to a deepened understanding of effective CPD and its impact and gave rise to many interesting and exciting projects, a selection of which we have written up as case studies of effective practice.

Impact evaluation

The TDA states that it's important to be clear about the key principles underlying effective evaluation of the impact of CPD. It makes reference to eight principles, including the importance of planning, focusing on what participants learn, and agreeing the evidence base and the success criteria for the evaluation of impact (TDA, 2007; http://www.tda.gov.uk/upload/resources/pdf/i/impact_evaluation. pdf).

Evaluating the impact of CPD is an aspect of the 'logical chain' or learning and development cycle that many educational leaders struggle with, and they are looking for practical and simple ways to achieve this. The approach to impact evaluation developed by the LCLL was used to underpin the *Effective Practices in CPD* project.

A useful overview of relevant literature on the evaluation of CPD is given by Bubb and Earley (2007). They cite Kirkpatrick's early work on impact evaluation (1959), which identified impact on four levels: reactions; learning; behaviour; outcomes. Thomas Guskey (2000) introduced a significant focus on evaluating CPD through 'learning outcomes' for young people. Guskey sees impact as being achieved at five potential levels:

- participants' reactions
- participants' learning
- organisation support and change
- participants' use of new knowledge and skills
- student learning outcomes.

Crucially, he argues that all five levels of impact are necessary if the goal of improving classroom learning is to be achieved.

Subsequently, Goodall et al. (2005) investigated the range of evaluative practices for CPD in a sample of schools in England. Using Guskey's five levels as a framework, they found that schools lacked the experience, skills and tools to evaluate the impact of CPD. Consequently, 'the impact of CPD on student learning was rarely evaluated by schools in the study and if done so, was rarely executed very effectively or well' (see Porritt, 2009, p.8). *The Logical Chain* came to the same conclusion: 'Few schools evaluated the impact of CPD on teaching and learning successfully' (Ofsted, 2006, p.2). As noted above, in 2007 the TDA published eight principles for impact evaluation which built on the above frameworks, and the most recent study by Bubb and Earley (2010) makes reference to 12 different levels of impact from any development activity.

We therefore have a range of models and frameworks, yet school and CPD leaders are reluctant to employ such tools effectively. Evaluation of CPD seems to be stuck at the first level of participant reactions ('happy sheets'), and organisations and leaders are unsure how to move past this. Another concern is that impact evaluation often focuses on CPD activity – what has happened – rather than on the difference the development activity makes for the participants and the young people with whom they work – the change that has been brought about.

Many people think of CPD as activities to be engaged in rather than as the actual development of their knowledge and expertise, which may (or may not) result from their participation in such activities. CPD is seen in terms of inputs and not as the changes effected in their thinking and practice. There is little reference to outcomes – what will happen as a result of development activity. An obstacle to a better appreciation of the impact of CPD lies in the way that it is conventionally defined – hence the need for a more comprehensive definition, such as that provided earlier. CPD is not one activity or set of activities; it is not definable as a course, a series of courses, a programme of learning or study, or even as a set of learning experiences. Rather, professional development may result from any or all of these activities and from the individual's reflection on their day-to-day experience of doing the job (Bubb and Earley, 2010).

LCLL's approach to impact evaluation is a very practical one that is simple in concept yet rigorous in the difference it can make. The initial thinking behind this approach was first highlighted in *London's Learning* (Porritt, 2005; Porritt et al., 2006). This resource explored Guskey's key concept that:

> *Good evaluation does not need to be complex; what is necessary is good planning and paying attention to evaluation at the outset of the professional development program, not at the end.*
>
> (Guskey, 2000, p.x)

Traditional impact evaluation tends to take place at the end of a development activity. We believe that 'all initial planning as to the potential impact of CPD should be undertaken *before* CPD activity starts' (Porritt, 2009, p.8). By 'impact' we mean, for example, stating *specific* changes in a teacher's classroom strategies or clarifying a changed approach towards children in the playground by a lunchtime supervisor. In terms of learning outcomes, we must agree at the outset the differences in how children learn as a result of proposed CPD activity – for example, 'pupils will move from using closed questions to the use of higher order questioning'. This is a simple concept to agree, yet requires a significant change in the CPD practice of many organisations.

We need to know what sort of impact we are looking for and participants in the *Effective Practices in CPD* project were encouraged to look at impact evaluation in terms of three separate yet related areas: *products, processes* and *outcomes (impact)*. Products might include policies or resources. Processes are new or improved systems. But do they really make a difference to colleagues and children and young people? We argued that the key was to plan the expected specific impact at the outset, which involves having a clear picture of what things are like before engaging in CPD activity so that there is a baseline against which to evaluate progress.

Let us look at these three separate yet related areas – *products, processes* and *outcomes* – in more detail.

Products can be seen as a focus on tangible outputs from development work, e.g. an improved policy, a new strategy document, a directory/database of available CPD opportunities, a newsletter, an ICT tool to support performance management, a workshop, the creation of a development programme, the establishment of a network meeting, production of consortium action plans, etc.

Processes are the *new or improved systems* in the schools, e.g. improved alignment between CPD and performance management, investigating what aspects of CPD staff feel to be effective, full involvement of staff in CPD processes, development of new knowledge and skills, creation of a new approach to needs analysis, etc.

However, do products and processes really articulate the *impact* of CPD on staff and pupils? We suggest that impact can best be seen in terms of the difference that is made by using the product or experiencing the process to *the learning and the experience* of colleagues, the teams and the school, and therefore to the learning and experience of the children and young people.

For example, producing a new CPD directory – a *product* – has the *potential* to have an *impact*, but creating the directory is not what makes the difference. Rather, it is how staff feel about and use the opportunities which the directory creates (*process*) that may make a difference. The *outcome* would be the difference their feelings or newly developed practice makes to their teaching or the way they carry out their role and, ultimately, the difference this makes to the learning and experience of the children.

This difference can best be expressed as *impact*. It is often harder to quantify this difference, yet it is important to be able to say how you know you are making or have made a difference.

So we suggest the key questions for impact evaluation are:

- What have we achieved (as a result of engaging in CPD activity) that is making a difference to the practice of the staff, the school and to the learning of the children?
- What evidence is telling us that we are making this difference?

Impact is the difference in staff behaviours, attitudes, skills and practice as a result of the professional development in which staff have engaged. Ultimately, impact is also the difference in the learning and experience of the children and young people as a result of the change in staff practice. Bringing about an improved outcome in the learning and experience of the children is what enables us to say that professional development of staff has been effective.

In the second phase of the project we drew upon the work of Frost and Durrant (2003) and the TDA (2006) to better understand the impact the project was having on staff and pupil outcomes. We distinguished between three sorts of impact on staff: classroom practice, personal capacity and interpersonal capacity. Project leaders were asked to identify any differences in staff knowledge, behaviours, attitudes, skills and capacity as a result of development activities using the headings classroom practice, personal capacity and interpersonal capacity (see Table 1.1).

Table 1.1

Classroom practice
Changes in subject/process knowledge
Changes in classroom practice

Personal capacity
Improved existing skills/practice
Learned new skills/practice
Change in staff confidence and self-esteem
More positive attitudes/behaviours
Happier and more motivated
Improved reflection on practice
Greater ability to take part in/lead change initiatives

Interpersonal capacity
More effective ways of working together
Changes in the practice of colleagues
More confidence in sharing good practice and managing and influencing colleagues
Greater willingness and ability to contribute productively to debate in staff meetings
Greater ability to question alternative viewpoints

To ascertain any differences in the learning and experience of the children and therefore to enable the project leaders to say that the development of their staff had been effective, we asked for evidence in relation to the following impact on children:

- enjoyment in learning
- attitudes

- participation
- pride in and organisation of work
- response to questions and tasks
- performance and progress
- engagement in a wider range of learning activities.

It was important for projects to be very clear on the original practice that they wished to improve so that they were then able to articulate the difference that had been achieved as a result of engaging in CPD. Examples of products, processes and outcomes (impact) are given below.

Table 1.2: LCLL's example for impact evaluation for the Effective Practices in CPD project

Focus of CPD project: Early professional development (EPD)

1. Products

Baseline: Our original practice was:	Impact: Our improved practice will be:
• Teachers in their early years feel that they lack access to CPD opportunities *as seen by* informal comments they make to the CPD leader.	• To produce a directory of CPD opportunities for teachers in years 2–5 of their career *as seen by* its placement on the school's shared directory.

2. Processes

Baseline: Our original practice was:	Impact: Our improved practice will be:
• Early career teachers (ECTs) feel that their individual development needs are not seen as important by the school *as seen by* comments made in exit interviews of teachers who have left the school.	• To develop a system by end of summer term (ready for implementation in the autumn term) in which EPD teachers are entitled to, and can access, at least one personalised development opportunity per term *as seen by* scrutiny of the team/school CPD records or in discussion with the teacher.

3. Impact/Outcomes

Baseline: What we were doing originally:	Impact: The impact we will have:
• Teachers in years 2–5 of their career find it difficult to say how their involvement in CPD has improved their assessment for learning (AfL) practice in the classroom and the learning of the children *as seen by* responses to this question in performance management discussions.	• Teachers in years 2–5 of their career can articulate how pupils used newly acquired higher order questioning skills as a result of the change in their teaching practice due to engagement in two AfL workshops. This can be *seen by* their sharing of this practice in team meetings.

Our approach to impact evaluation requires knowing what the position is at the outset (baseline) and what it will look like afterwards, as a result of the CPD activity or practice. This requires clarifying the evidence which supports the baseline and will demonstrate impact at the planning stage. To assist a better understanding of this approach, examples of baseline and impact evidence were offered to the project leaders (see below).

Example 1

1a: The project baseline was:
Prior to this project, information regarding the impact of support staff on teaching and learning was patchy. It appeared as if levels of confidence and understanding of their potential to make a difference varied significantly between different groups of support staff and individuals.

1b: The evidence that supported the project baseline was:
Little hard evidence was available. Prior to this project, information regarding the impact of support staff on teaching and learning was very anecdotal and disparate.

2a: The impact picture at the end of the project is:
Our improved practice is shown in the support staff meetings, where there is a clearer understanding of strategies that can be used and the influence support staff have in improving classroom practice. Our CPD sessions in practising the delivery of difficult messages have enabled support staff to be proactive in tackling issues they might previously have avoided. There is now a shared understanding and vocabulary around good lessons and teaching. Sharing some of their key perceptions about good lessons with the whole staff group has helped to raise the status of support staff and highlighted their potential to make a positive difference in the classroom.

2b: The evidence that shows this impact is:
Evidence was derived from discussions with staff *(include examples of quotations)* and from a questionnaire administered to all support staff who were involved in the project. This showed that more support staff were expressing confidence in their ability to tackle difficult messages: this increased from about one-fifth at the start of the project to about two-thirds at the end.

Example 2

1a: The project baseline was:
Following the well-structured NQT induction period, which involved coaching and mentoring, early professional development for early career teachers often meant attending courses. Professional learning conversations were limited within the departmental structure and there was little opportunity to seek guidance and support from other colleagues. Few colleagues were objectively able to identify their strengths and areas for development based upon the Professional Standards or to articulate these with supportive evidence. These were only reviewed when performance management arose. Subsequently staff felt classroom practice was good, but didn't take risks or 'put things off'. In addition, early career teachers did not appreciate their relevance to the wider school context and were very inward-looking.

1b: The evidence that supported the project baseline was:
Evidence was derived from conversations with staff and via performance management interviews.

2a: The impact picture at the end of the project is:
We have developed a coaching system and established a formal network to enable early career teachers to develop areas of identified practice. The first stage has been the use of a self-review process (on-line via BLUE), facilitated by a coach. This has enabled our nine early career teachers to establish specific strengths and areas for development, supported by the Professional Standards. Colleagues have been able to engage in a professional learning conversation around the Standards, ensuring a more rigorous, objective focus on their practice.

The use of BLUE and support of coaches has ensured that all early career teachers were able to clearly identify their strengths and produce resources to support their colleagues' practice, attaching these to teaching standards. Once strengths and development needs had been identified with coaches, they came together to create a matrix to establish support needs, with a strong focus on cross-school collaboration. Via short conferences, coaches themselves also provided presentations in which they gave exemplar 'best practice' sessions for the early career teachers. One area in which a number of coaches from different schools collaborated was in the support of national Standard C13, identified by the majority of early career teachers as an area of development need.

2b: The evidence that shows this impact is:
Presentations led by the ECTs provided evidence of very significant developments in their learning and in their evaluation of that process. ECTs were able to share their initial learning at two learning conferences and show how this did (or was going to) impact on their classroom practice. In the Q&A sessions that followed their presentations, questions asked demonstrated the development of thinking around the topics presented and transferred from subject to subject.

Feedback from ECTs demonstrates that all have made significant progress. Their final reviews with their coaches indicate significant development in practice. Feedback from lesson observations shows that seven of the nine ECTs improved their ability to use data to ensure clear progress by pupils over a unit of work (national Standard C13). The teachers have appreciated the project. One said, 'I like the feeling that I have been listened to and that my ideas are being put forward'; another said, 'It is helpful to know that I am experiencing similar barriers as others'.

Such initial planning and thinking about impact leads naturally to some rigorous questioning. The answers to these questions help an organisation, team or individual to design an approach that offers some practical solutions. In particular we believe 'establishing the current practice or *baseline* is vital to help colleagues articulate the quality and depth of the subsequent *impact* on adult practice and young people's learning' (Porritt, 2009).

The questions we encouraged projects to explore included:

- What is impact evaluation? Why should we do it?
- What is your current practice, your baseline? What is the evidence to show this?
- For whom do you want professional development to make a difference?
- By when?
- Does it make a positive difference? How much of a difference?
- How do we know? What is the evidence of impact?
- How can we evaluate impact simply and practically?

Working on such questions with schools, local authorities and CPD leaders has led to the evolution of this simple yet innovative approach to impact evaluation. Our approach to impact evaluation, which was used in the TDA-funded project, enabled projects to design improvement and development processes that were more effective and had greater potential to ensure impact was achieved. Evaluating the impact of CPD in this way is a powerful method to raise the quality of learning and standards, with value for money and accountability being helpful additions. Educational organisations tend to view impact evaluation as being about demonstrating external accountability and so have not looked at making innovations in this field. If we see impact evaluation as a high-quality learning tool, we can bring about a step change in its application. This was partially achieved in the TDA-funded project, and it is to the main findings that we now turn.

Main findings

The *Effective Practices in CPD* project was very successful in meeting its aims. Just over 90 per cent of project leaders rated their project as 'successful' or 'very successful'. Of those providing information, not a single project rated itself as 'unsuccessful'.

In phase 1 of the project we identified the following elements as crucial to achieving success:

- identifcation of effective and realistic aims at the outset
- the development of staff knowledge and skills
- a focus on pupil achievement
- the engagement and motivation of individuals involved
- positive support from one or more members of the senior leadership team
- provision of resources, i.e. time, money
- external stimulus provided by local authorities, HEIs, other schools or agencies
- strong project management.

Positive outcomes included: better attitudes towards CPD; engagement with a wider variety of CPD opportunities; hitherto reluctant staff volunteering to take on roles and responsibilities; and increasing involvement of support staff in CPD activity.

Many projects explored coaching as a way of engaging in effective CPD practice. During phase 1, this tended to focus on developing coaching skills and putting newly found skills into practice. Development opportunities focused on classroom activity, such as lesson observation. Enquiry-based approaches were less common. Collaborative approaches to CPD were a regular feature of the projects: the most successful were seen in established partnerships such as those supported by a local authority. Other projects used phase 1 to establish the logistics and aims of a new partnership and were not able to move on to explore collaborative CPD in the time frame available.

By the end of the project's first phase we identified nine factors that we felt underpinned the most successful projects and strongly influenced effective CPD practice. These were:

- establishing clarity of purpose at the outset in CPD activity
- specifying a focus and goal for CPD activity, aligned to clear timescales
- including a focus on pupil outcomes in CPD activity
- ensuring participants' ownership of CPD activity
- engaging with a variety of CPD opportunities
- including time for reflection and feedback
- ensuring collaborative approaches to CPD
- developing strategic leadership of CPD
- understanding how to evaluate the impact of CPD.

Project leaders were asked to build on their progress from the first phase by selecting one or more of the above factors to help them embed and refine their project work. The evidence from both phases was that the above *CPD approaches* were determining factors in ensuring that CPD activity had an impact on colleagues' thinking and practice, the learning of pupils and organisational improvement.

In the second phase of the project, the CPD activity highlighted was as wide ranging as in phase 1. However, the CPD activities which dominated the second phase were those that offered the greatest potential for impact in the classroom and across the school according to the research synthesis from the Evidence for Policy and Practice Information and Co-ordinating Centre (EPPI) and summed up in TDA guidance (TDA, 2008). Developmental lesson observation and action research were more common CPD activities in phase 2 than in the first phase. Coaching was seen as very effective and, overall, it was the most commonly used CPD activity, with the project funding stimulating many organisations to explore and adopt coaching within their CPD provision. It should be noted that projects that adopted a judicious combination of CPD activity reported a stronger culture shift within their organisation, particularly when coaching was adopted following engagement with CPD activity. This suggests a shift from coaching as a CPD activity in itself to coaching being used to support and embed learning from other CPD activity.

Over both phases of the project, it was clear there had been a significant cultural change within some organisations as a result of involvement in the *Effective Practices in CPD project*. The project stimulated involvement of support staff in CPD activity within project organisations. Project leaders indicated improvements in classroom practice and subject knowledge. There were also suggestions of significant improvements in honing existing and developing new skills, staff confidence and reflection. Project leaders were very positive about their desire to carry forward and develop project gains, and the experience of the project had helped to (re)ignite a latent passion for CPD as a key enabler for school change and improvement.

A clear gain from the project has been learning around successes and challenges in evaluating the impact of CPD, both for project participants and the TDA. The clear and rigorous evaluative framework we provided, supported and challenged projects to develop their thinking and practice about what effective CPD was, how to achieve this and how to evaluate the impact of CPD activity. The monitoring and evaluative framework and the need to think through a project for the LCLL consultants to scrutinise was helpful for the focus of many of the project leaders. Greater use was made of a variety of methods to gather impact data and increasing numbers of projects were able to identify what they were learning from that evidence and demonstrate greater clarity about improvements they wanted to achieve. In phase 2 there was more use of evidence from pupils, showing a greater awareness of the impact of CPD on learning. Many projects sought and used evaluation evidence to track progress rather than regard impact evaluation as an end-of-project process.

It was also clear however that considerable development would still be needed to ensure that the understanding of the majority of the project leaders matched that of the most successful in terms of the key principles of impact evaluation.

Project leaders were enthusiastic about what had been achieved and most were planning to continue to build on the progress already made, to embed and consolidate by formalising processes. Many were expanding to involve more staff or other schools or to extend the professional learning to other environments, locations and contexts. Projects were very positive about their desire to carry forward and develop the gains made. Some referred to a legacy of goodwill and noted the significant impact of their project. Projects were grateful for the funding that supported their work but, while totally appreciative of this, they were more genuinely enthused by the outcomes and benefits of being involved in a national project to develop knowledge, practice, policy and strategy in CPD. They recognised that they had been given a unique opportunity and that the funding and involvement in the project had enabled them to make a significant shift in their practices and, in some cases, in the whole-school culture as a result.

In conclusion, there was strong evidence to suggest that real change in CPD thinking, practice and culture had been achieved through involving schools and other organisations in testing, trialling, exploring and evaluating approaches to CPD. The sample of case studies from the *Effective Practices in CPD* project in Part 2 of this book provides some illustrations of these changes.

The structure of the book

This edited collection is made up of three parts: the introductory chapter, the case studies and the concluding chapter. Part 2 – Case studies of practice – constitutes the bulk of the book (Chapters 2 to 11). Each case study outlines the gains for the project participants in terms of their exploration of effective CPD practices. The case studies focus on the projects' experiences and their journey towards effective CPD practice, exploring what they were trying to achieve, how successful they were (and, importantly, how they knew they were successful) and what were some of the challenges of the journey. The case studies make specific reference to the nine factors or approaches to CPD identified earlier as underpinning effective practice.

In the concluding chapter we attempt to summarise the lessons learned from the TDA-funded project and consider the future of CPD within the context of an evolving and rapidly developing field, the growing focus on CPD leadership and the national strategy for school workforce development led by the TDA.

Part 2

Case studies of practice

Introduction

It was always the intention to produce some case studies from the *Effective Practices in Continuing Professional Development* project, both to inform the TDA's strategic thinking and for a more general readership. A total of 20 were written for the TDA and a sample of these has been selected for this volume.

The original case studies were chosen using a range of criteria. The regional consultants from the London Centre for Leadership in Learning (LCLL), who were supporting and monitoring the 152 projects, were asked to select projects from their region that they thought would make interesting case studies. Having drawn up a longlist of potential case studies, we as project directors examined each project carefully, taking into account a range of selection criteria such as geographical location, phase, setting, type of project and focus area. The main purpose of the case studies was to describe and analyse the journeys that the projects had made: what were their starting points and baselines; how far had they progressed (and how did they measure that progress); what were important milestones on the way; and what impact had they achieved?

We wished to explore what had been learned as a result of their participation in the TDA-funded project, and how this related to what we know about effective CPD and the evaluation of its impact. We knew that the experience of some projects had been very significant; participation has helped to change organisational culture, improve their practice and has led to a deepened understanding of effective CPD and its evaluation. We wished to document that experience and record the key learning points on their journey to more effective CPD practice and a learning-centred culture.

In producing the case studies the consultants were asked to collect information about the project from a variety of sources: project application forms, data capture forms and end-of-project reports which had used a template we'd provided. Primary data were also collected through site visits, during which time interviews were conducted which mapped the learning journey, the main challenges and lessons learned, and the impact of the projects. Most of the information was derived from conversations with project leaders, but case study evidence was also gathered from a range of people, such as teachers, support staff and, occasionally, pupils.

The consultants were asked to adopt a critical stance and ask probing questions about the participants' experiences and their journeys towards effective practice. For example, what were they trying to achieve, how successful had they been, and what were some of the successes and challenges of the journey? The case study writers critically examined the lessons learned and what they thought was needed for the projects to achieve greater success. They did this with specific reference to the nine factors and approaches to effective CPD that were outlined in Part 1.

Case study writers were asked to comment on the specific *impact* of the projects. However, the case studies were never intended to be examples of projects that got everything right in terms of the nine approaches or factors; rather it was felt it would be valuable to document a range of projects, including those that were less successful, in order to see what lessons could be learned.

The case studies selected for this volume begin with Carol Taylor's account of a project that was concerned with developing teaching and learning by focusing on the features of best practice. It involved three secondary schools working together to design and run a programme which aimed to develop 'outstanding' teachers who were seen as central to school improvement. Although it was too early to judge the impact of the programme, the collaboration between the headteachers of the schools had been a significant factor in the project's success. Each headteacher recognised the others' strengths and expertise and used this to full advantage. Participants from the partnership schools said that the programme had made a significant difference to them in a number of ways.

Chapter 3, by Sara Bubb, is an interesting account of how one secondary school attempted, with varying degrees of success, to build on the successes of the project's first phase to introduce an action learning approach to practitioner enquiry across the whole school. It was a very ambitious project, which aimed to help the school become more 'research engaged' and it offers many learning points regarding effective staff development.

Chapter 4, by John Tandy, concerns a network of primary schools working across two local authorities who wished to evaluate the impact of their extended provision. The project enabled the network to do this and succeeded in enhancing the professional knowledge, skills and understanding, and confidence of staff who engaged with the project. Support staff who participated developed a greater understanding of how they contributed to the extended services work of the school and how extended provision complemented the work of the official school day and contributed to the schools' overall success.

The next three chapters all cover coaching as a means of improving practice. Chapter 5, by Vivienne Porritt, investigates how coaching was used in a secondary school to improve teaching and learning, and to develop leadership capacity. Initially the school did not see coaching as a high-status activity and it was not being used to bring about performance improvements. An outcome of the project was an increased sense among staff of belonging to a professional learning community and being involved in improvements in practice. It enabled the school to develop a stronger and more reflective approach to professional learning and the school reported increased participation among leaders at all levels in whole-school strategic leadership. The term 'coaching conversation' became part of the language of leadership within the school and leaders now report that 'CPD and coaching has become such an accepted part of the way we do things here'.

The project 'Developing coaching as an effective method of CPD', reported in Chapter 6 by Steve Illingworth, aimed to develop a culture of coaching in secondary schools across a local authority. In so doing, a model was produced which helped assess the impact of CPD on both the practice of teachers and on the standards of pupil learning in the classroom. As in the previous case study, one of the main challenges faced by the project was to raise the status of coaching as an effective CPD activity in the eyes of teachers, particularly senior leaders. Within the context of a monitoring culture, it was a challenge to establish professional development activity such as coaching, which is essentially reflective, non-judgemental and developmental. Teachers and senior leaders have increasingly realised that coaching is excellent CPD because it is sustainable, self-reflective and impacts directly on classroom practice.

Chapter 7, written by Sara Bubb, is a case study of coaching in a special school. Staff in the school were trained in coaching using the GROW model. This fitted in well with the school's approach to helping students manage their behaviour because it was about them making choices about pursuing different courses of action. The evaluation of the project made use of a 'causation trail' that starts with performance management or appraisal and ends with the review of impact. There was a desire to make teachers and support staff feel more valued because of the investment in them and to make coaching sustainable by developing expert coaching at the school rather than relying on external coaching.

The next chapter, by Margaret Mulholland, focuses on a primary school that wanted to develop its staff in the teaching of maths and support the mathematical thinking and reasoning of pupils. The project inspired staff and resulted in far more collaborative learning and problem-solving approaches being used in classes. Although more work was needed, it was acknowledged that as a result of the project the school was now closer to becoming a 'conjecturing community' where the teacher did not step in too quickly to provide the right answer, but rather allowed the children to question, make suggestions and be guided towards working out problems for themselves. External consultants had been used, but the school staff now had the confidence and the expertise to take this learning forward. The project helped the school to identify that it had the internal expertise and capacity to lead CPD.

Chapter 9, by Sara Bubb, is a case study of a secondary school that wished to develop more effective CPD evaluation in order to improve the quality of future CPD, with the aim of raising staff job satisfaction and pupil achievement. Although the school had strong staff development, the CPD leader felt that evaluating its impact was a weak link and so this was the priority throughout the project. There were two development initiatives that were specifically implemented and monitored for impact: professional development for early career teachers, and development for classroom-based support staff. The project compared staff's and students' perceptions of progress over time. This showed that the staff's perception of the occurrence of good practices was greater than that of the students. The school still has some way to go, but it is getting there and has significantly increased its understanding of impact evaluation.

The key aim of the project reported in Chapter 10 by Steve Lloyd was to develop a professional development framework to which all staff could subscribe, to measure performance and identify areas of future development. It aimed to engage teachers and TAs in classroom-based 'change' projects based on needs identified by the National Standards. The project helped the development of an open and honest culture, allowing issues such as status and hierarchy to be challenged and developed. Not only was the style of CPD provision addressed but so also were some of the underlying cultural issues. Greater self-confidence and a wider range of skills among colleagues were noted, as was an improved feeling of teamwork as the staff members developed a greater understanding and appreciation of each other's roles. Pupils too were showing a different attitude to the adults they worked with, regarding teachers, TAs and others as people who can and do help them with their learning.

The final chapter, by John Tandy, is a fascinating account of how leadership practices in primary schools in a local authority were developed. The project had a significant impact on the thinking and practice of participants and influenced networking and collaborative practice among primary headteachers. It made use of 'enquiry walks' – a school-based appreciative enquiry programme that enables an aspect of a school or a particular theme of professional learning to be viewed and evaluated in practice. The collaborative working also contributed to a Leadership Learning Charter, which encapsulated key principles of effective leadership within the local authority.

Chapter 2

Developing teaching and learning

Carol Taylor

Context

This project involved three secondary schools. The lead school, which became a specialist sports college in 2004, is an oversubscribed 11–18 school with nearly 2,000 pupils in a locality where there is selection. The proportion of children eligible for free school meals is low, while the proportion of those with learning difficulties and/or disabilities as well as those with a statement of special educational need is higher than the national average. The school and its last Ofsted inspection in 2008 acknowledged that:

> A broad range of staff development is raising the quality of teaching and learning, which is now good with some examples of outstanding practice... Through an effective professional development programme, teaching and learning is now good overall... and a comprehensive programme of lesson observations and training is beginning to raise standards in the classroom, and processes for monitoring students' performance are being embedded... although 'green shoots' are starting to emerge, sufficient impact of many of the initiatives cannot yet be seen.

The headteacher in the lead school is passionate about the professional development of the whole staff and is clear that this is key to further whole-school improvement. The head has moved the school from special measures (when GCSE results were around 32 per cent A–C) to the current position where in 2007 55 per cent of students achieved A–C. The key focus of school improvement is on the quality of teaching and learning and is based on the firm belief that all pupils are entitled to the highest quality teaching. Consequently the school's CPD programme is central to driving this focus forward.

The teaching staff have their professional development needs identified through the school's performance management process where reviewers map the teachers' career path and identify individual CPD needs, which are in line with whole-school and faculty objectives. In phase 1 of the project, performance management reviewers engaged in professional development with an external consultancy to better enable them to effectively coach and support the staff. All of the support staff and wider workforce have a performance management programme similar to that of the teaching staff, but it is recognised that there is still work to do in this area.

Classroom-based action research projects have enabled 15 teaching staff to implement and assess a range of teaching and learning strategies with support from the school's advanced skills teacher. In addition, an external coach was made available through the General Teaching Council's Teacher Learning Academy (GTC TLA) programme. The school has gained GTC TLA Centre status, which has enabled some of the staff to become verifiers and so support the work of their own colleagues as well as teachers from other schools. There is an extensive twilight CPD programme led by staff and organised to enable the teachers and teaching assistants to attend a range of development sessions on four key areas: general teaching, assessment for learning, middle leadership, and aspiring senior leaders.

The school has now established an early professional development (EPD) coaching programme where staff new to the profession map and discuss their career paths and so achieve both personal and professional stability as well as an understanding of the Professional Standards and how to progress to Threshold.

Prior to their current engagement with the *Effective Practices in CPD* project, the school had also been involved in a TDA Partnership Development programme. This funded project focused on increasing the school's capacity for initial teacher training (ITT) placements. By working in partnership with a university, the school now has a number of staff who have gained the local provider's mentor qualification.

Where appropriate, other staff are supported through the National College for Leadership of Schools and Children's Service's National Professional Qualification for Headship (NPQH), Leadership Pathways and Leading from the Middle programmes. The school is also a Microsoft Academy and a number of staff have gained internationally recognised qualifications.

Feedback from the staff suggests that they enjoy the opportunity to share their practice with colleagues, that CPD is highly valued and that there is a culture of openness, sharing and trust and a real sense that the learning of the adults in the organisation is key to improving the learning of the pupils.

Phase 1 project

The lead school continued to make progress and improve the standards of learning and teaching identified at the time of the project's commencement (that about two-thirds of lessons were good to outstanding). The senior leadership team (SLT) in the lead school felt that middle leadership was key to moving the school forward and that middle leaders who were effective coaches would be more able to support the development of their colleagues and teams and so improve the quality of teaching and learning. There was no in-house professional development programme in place to cater for the specific needs of middle leaders and there had been no professional development opportunities to develop coaching strategies across this key group.

Aims

The aims of the phase 1 project were to achieve:

- a new management development programme that would develop middle leader confidence and clarity about the role
- middle leader coaching skills to enable them to better support others
- sharing of good and outstanding practice across the school
- a 10 per cent increase in 'outstanding' teacher performance in the classroom and a whole-school increase of 15 per cent of 'good or better' observed lessons
- a more robust career path for senior and middle leaders to progress, using the new national professional standards
- a more supportive culture that would improve retention rates of middle leaders.

The strategies identified to meet the above aims were:

- middle and senior leaders observed all teaching staff in pairs, using Ofsted criteria as part of an internal coaching programme
- staff feedback clearly identified areas for development and good and outstanding teaching
- all performance management reviewers and middle leaders engaged in professional development in coaching skills with an external coach, using nationally recognised assessment coaching criteria
- senior leaders coached middle leaders through the observation process
- the new Professional Standards were adapted and effectively used by senior and middle leaders to map and enhance their career paths
- using this model across the whole school and sharing it with other schools involved in the Partnership Development programme.

Impact of phase 1

The classification of CPD into products, processes and outcomes was used to identify the project's baseline position and the impact gained.

Products

Baseline: original practice was:

- Middle leaders were saying that they lacked guidance in the leadership aspect of their role.

Impact: improved practice was:

- The design and implementation of a comprehensive leadership programme for middle leaders.

Processes

Baseline: original practice was:

- Middle leaders were saying that their leadership needs were not seen as important by the school, as evidenced by discussion with senior management.

Impact: improved practice was:

- The development of a rolling leadership programme that enabled all middle leaders to understand their role.
- Specific CPD sessions targeted at aspiring leaders, middle leaders and senior leaders.
- A comprehensive coaching programme put in place to support established middle leaders.

Outcomes/impact

Baseline: original practice was:

- Senior staff observed a lack of consistency in terms of middle leader behaviours. Through discussions with senior leaders it became apparent that middle leaders did not have a clear understanding of their roles and responsibilities and so were individually interpreting what was required of them.

Impact: improved practice was:

- Middle leaders now understood the context of their leadership role and agreed on a consistent set of behaviours to demonstrate these expectations.

- Middle leaders now engaged in senior leadership team (SLT) meetings to discuss whole-school issues and agreed to lead four whole-school focus groups.

As a result of the programme middle leaders shared their feelings:

> We feel respected – the external venue and facilitation made us feel as if we are being treated professionally.

> It has helped to clarify our leadership role and we enjoyed spending time together and agreeing a consistent group approach.

Middle leaders agreed that they needed to embrace coaching as an approach to further develop the culture of the school and acknowledged their role in improving standards, meeting with the SLT once a month to discuss whole-school issues. They also led four focus groups or teams:

- Leading learning (heads of faculty)
- Teaching and learning
- Behaviour for learning
- Literacy for learning.

A further outcome of the project was the development of a CPD portfolio that embeds the professional teaching standards within a personalised professional development programme.

Phase 2 project

The school changed the focus of their work in the second phase of the project. Originally, they had intended to focus on embedding middle leader competencies, implementing the professional standards, middle leader coaching skills and innovative learning and teaching practices that linked to outstanding teaching and learning. However, it was decided that informal leaders (those without a formal title but who were involved in whole school activities such as mentoring newly qualified teachers (NQTs) or leading aspects of the school professional development programme) also had a key role to play, especially in respect of embedding outstanding practices across the school. As a result of the observation programme established in phase 1, the school was able to identify where consistently outstanding practice was happening. It was also felt that continuing the collaboration between schools in similar circumstances would help to build a pool of expertise, and develop capacity and sustainability across the local authority. The additional two partnership schools are also schools facing challenging circumstances, but where Ofsted had also recognised that there were some examples of outstanding practice.

Aim

The development of a tailored in-house professional development programme for outstanding teachers.

The baseline picture at the commencement of phase 2 was as follows:

- Whole school: outstanding teaching had been identified through the school's internal lesson observation cycle. Good and outstanding lessons had shifted from 65 per cent at the start of phase 1 to 72 per cent at the end of phase 1.
- The three participants selected for the programme were recognised by the SLT in the lead school as teachers who were consistently teaching good and outstanding lessons. One was involved in mentoring NQTs and beginning teachers, one had been acting head of department and all had been involved in leading whole school professional development activities.
- There was no specific CPD opportunity for outstanding teachers.
- The school had strong partnerships and collaboration with other schools in the local authority.
- The individuals knew that they were consistently teaching good and outstanding lessons, but did not have a whole-school role in leading teaching and learning and were not always confident about or understood why they were 'outstanding'. They said, for example:

What makes an outstanding lesson? I want clarity about what outstanding teaching is and what it looks like.

Before the programme I did not have the confidence to say anything at team meetings and would think colleagues might say 'What does she know about this' or 'What makes her think that she knows what she is talking about' and so I would not say anything.

I knew that I was teaching consistently well, but was wondering 'Where next for me?' I was ready for another challenge but wanted to stay focused on the classroom and not on moving to middle leadership.

The project's plan and objectives were:

- to create a tailored 'Outstanding Teacher' (OT) programme that will meet the needs of the lead and partnership schools and ensure that outstanding teaching is recognised, embedded and shared
- to ensure that outstanding teachers are more confident and secure in their own practice and are better able to lead learning across their teams
- to ensure that outstanding teachers will develop coaching skills such that they are better able to coach others to achieve outstanding teaching
- to work with a partnership of two other schools with a view to creating a pool of outstanding teachers that can be shared across the partnership
- to identify and support aspiring leaders who can step into more formal leadership roles.

The leadership for the project changed in the second phase when the headteacher took the leading role, working closely with the assistant head/CPD leader.

The Outstanding Teacher programme was created in partnership and constituted the following elements:

- three outstanding teachers from each of the three collaborating schools
- six sessions facilitated by the headteacher of the lead school, and an external consultant and former headteacher
- a mixture of facilitated teaching and learning sessions, coaching and mentoring and optional planning towards advanced skills teacher (AST) status.

The outstanding teachers were identified in a number of ways. The lead school worked collaboratively with a number of schools in the local authority to develop the necessary people skills and expertise to create a teaching and learning audit. The audit creates a model that is used as the vehicle to explore outstanding teaching and learning. It describes in detail what teachers do and what they need to reflect upon in order to be 'outstanding' and to remain outstanding by continually reflecting and updating their professional skills and competencies. The in-house programme that was created gave participants the opportunity to explore the teaching and learning audit and the implications for practice that it dictates.

Participants were identified as being 'outstanding teachers' by each of the three schools involved. Their outstanding practice extended beyond the classroom in that they were also excellent communicators who were considered to be role models for other teachers. In the lead school there was a rigorous selection process that used data from lesson observations together with existing data from line managers and the schools' rigorous recruitment process, senior leader observations and consideration of who were the change makers, or potential change makers, in the school.

What does the programme involve?

The teaching and learning audit is explored with the participants to help them clarify and define what can be expected of the teachers in their teams. Participants are taught how to use lesson observation and feedback for the improvement of colleagues across the school – and coaching skills are a key aspect of this.

The six sessions, made up of half- and full-day sessions, cover aspects of teaching and learning theories (such as Bloom and Piaget); the identification and exploration of the concept and practice of outstanding teaching; models of coaching and coaching skills, and, finally, a personalised 'next steps' plan.

The three participants interviewed said that, while they were 'excited and honoured' to be selected for the programme, they were also concerned about being 'singled out' and being exposed and vulnerable to their colleagues' expectations of 'outstanding'. However, the headteacher had decided that as this was a pilot programme he would protect the participants by not sharing with other colleagues the purpose, aims and objectives of the programme. This would also ensure that the next cohort of participants would not have preconceived ideas about the programme and would allow room for changes when the pilot was reviewed.

Although this strategy created some uncertainty among the participants, at the interviews they said they felt that it had enabled them to stay open-minded about the content and to 'find their own route through the learning journey' while not having to live up to any predetermined expectations. It also made the participants reflect on how the elements of the programme fitted together and what this meant for them.

Impact of phase 2

The first phase of the Outstanding Teacher programme did not finish until May 2009. This fact, coupled with the change in focus between the first to second phases, meant that it was too early to identify the impact the programme had had upon learning and teaching, on other colleagues and/or teams and upon the whole school. Future observations will potentially identify any impact on the quality of teaching and learning. However, there is some evidence of the impact of the programme upon the thinking of the individual participants and the beginnings of impact on individual practice.

Firsthand feedback from individuals was that they:

- felt valued and were eager to explore new teaching strategies with 'like-minded people'
- were challenged by the input on the programme, by the interaction with their colleagues and by the level of self-reflection required
- enjoyed the programme and the opportunity to rethink practice and pedagogy
- learnt how to be critical for the benefit of other colleagues
- were more confident in what they knew and in sharing this with others in their teams.

Participants said:

> This has been the best CPD I have ever been involved in – it has changed my life.

> I have already developed many of these ideas from the programme into my teaching.

This was endorsed by the line manager who said:

> My colleague has successfully been trying some really innovative approaches in assessment. Two pupils who rarely engage or produce any work completed it all and seemed to be engaged throughout the lesson and looked surprised when the lesson ended and said: 'Is that the end – it went really quickly!'

One participant said that being involved in the programme had enabled her to identify more clearly the 'outstanding' aspects of her teaching and to rethink what 'outstanding' actually meant. Another felt that she had already identified these elements and was in danger of 'teaching by rote', but the programme had enabled her to see that not only are there innovative ideas of which she was unaware but that a wider, whole-school role working with others would offer her the challenge that she was seeking. All the participants interviewed had come to their own realisation that they had a whole-school role to play in the future and this was something that they now felt enabled to do. To have been told that this was an expectation at the start of the programme would have made some of them anxious and 'exposed to failure'.

Participants from the partnership schools said that the programme made a significant difference to them.

> [It] changed my thinking totally. What I thought was outstanding has shifted and I now want to explore how I can continue to improve and in what ways.

> At first I felt very insecure – not knowing where we were going but I realise now how this works – the journey is mine but I am being guided along on the way.

Another noted:

> I realise that this is not just about me… I am now not going to be embarrassed any longer about being an outstanding teacher as there is a bigger picture. The coaching has helped me to see that I can make a difference to my team and to my school.

An associate head who was supporting one of the participating schools (which was in special measures) stated that the school had moved (using Ofsted categories) from 20 per cent of teaching being inadequate, 77 per cent being satisfactory/good and 2–3 per cent being outstanding, to a position where 50 per cent of teaching was now good and 12 per cent was outstanding. In his view, the partnership programme had supported that improvement. He intended to engage a further three teachers in the second-year programme, recognising that:

> I need nine outstanding teachers to tip the balance and so begin to make the difference across the whole school.

He stated that the programme had 'challenged participants and exposed them in a good way'. He reported that they were 'more buoyant', saying, 'I can't wait to get back and to help others do this.'

Overall judgement on the project's success

Clearly there were many aspects of good practice taking place within the project. However, concrete evidence of impact on the quality of teaching and learning was limited. The headteacher taking over the project did not have an understanding of the LCLL impact evaluation approach that was being explored. The Outstanding Teacher programme had only actually been in place for three months when the case study was written. Prior to this, the three partnership schools spent the time planning and writing the programme with the assistance of the coaching head who was also to be the second facilitator on the programme.

The collaboration between the headteachers of the schools was a significant factor in the success of the programme as they recognised each other's strengths and expertise and used this to full advantage.

The coaching session observed was of a very high quality and the participants were certainly extremely positive about it.

The partnership intends to continue to collaborate and offer a second year of the programme. They believed that the funding from the TDA enabled them to plan and deliver a tailored, high-quality and personalised professional development programme that had the potential to impact on school improvement across each of the three schools.

Features of effective professional development

- Establishing clarity of purpose at the outset in CPD activity

The project leader – in this case the headteacher and his team of second lead headteacher and the headteachers of the two partnerships schools – were very clear about the purpose of the project. However, they lacked understanding of the approach and format that could support evaluating the impact of CPD, i.e. the importance of baseline and impact statements with evidence.

There was clarity about the purpose and expected outcomes of the project. Not sharing this with the participants was a strategy adopted for a specific reason, i.e. to enable participants to work through their own learning journey without any preconceived ideas or expectations.

- Specifying a focus and goal for CPD activity aligned to clear timescales

The thorough planning of the project meant that the actual practice had only just begun at the time of the case study visit. This was in accordance with the expectations of the project team.

- Including a focus on pupil outcomes in CPD activity

The focus was on improving the quality of teaching and learning but, as yet, there was no evidence of this being achieved.

- Ensuring participants' ownership of CPD activity

Clearly, the school valued the opportunity to explore CPD activities that were considered to best meet their needs and their context. The individual participants were totally engaged with the programme and all of them had attended all sessions. The fact that the headteachers involved in the partnership were also committed ensured that the staff were released from classes to attend.

- Including time for reflection and feedback

It was very clear that participants had time to share their learning once back in their school – they were supported in this by the headteacher himself. The participants were also encouraged to practise their coaching skills with each other in order to embed their learning and also as a way of supporting each other.

- Ensuring collaborative approaches to CPD

This was considered to be extremely powerful – all the schools were in challenging circumstances and all recognised the importance of improving the quality of teaching in their schools and so the 'buy-in' from all partners was significant. Communication between partners was not an issue – as headteachers were the leads, they were able to ensure that time was found for planning and monitoring. All recognised the potential of creating a supportive network and shared resources, and they were anticipating using the participants between the partnership schools in the sense of 'home-grown' advanced skills teachers (ASTs).

- Developing strategic leadership of CPD

This was powerful, for all the reasons outlined above relating to the headteachers in each of the three schools strategically leading this professional development opportunity.

- Understanding how to evaluate the impact of CPD

The headteacher was new to leading this project and therefore had no understanding of the approach that had previously been adopted. There was no true baseline picture and evidence and, consequently, no true impact picture and evidence at the point of the project's completion.

Chapter 3

Engaging teachers in action research

Sara Bubb

Context

This project involved a very successful 11–18 secondary school: it was deemed outstanding by Ofsted in 2007 and for 14–19 provision in 2009. It exists in very challenging circumstances in that the number of students taking up free school meals, speaking languages other than English and with learning difficulties and disabilities is well above national average. Its contextual value added is one of the highest in the country.

This school has very strong staff development, which has been well led for many years. Its Ofsted report says, 'Leadership and learning are bound together in the sense that the adults in the college community are regarded as learners' (2007). The school is involved in many projects which bring with them extra funding. It has long held training school status and is an accredited provider with 20 places for the Graduate Teacher programme. Many CPD activities that are seen as cutting edge in other schools are well established here. For instance, there is a team of eight advanced skills teachers (ASTs) who support and develop staff. People have been part of the General Teaching Council Teacher Learning Academy (GTC TLA), and one teacher is accredited to award TLA levels 1 and 2. Observation of teaching is well established and there are three teaching spaces (a classroom, a gymnasium and a science laboratory) equipped with video cameras and microphones which enable mentors to communicate with teachers as lessons progress.

Phase 1 project

In such a school, it can be hard to know where to go next in order to further improve professional development. The deputy responsible for professional development felt that there were two areas which needed strengthening and saw the *Effective Practices in CPD* project as a means of doing this. They were:

- Provision for people in their second year of teaching who were feeling a little at sea after the strong organised support in their induction and training years.
- About a quarter of teachers had been or were engaged in action research or practitioner enquiry. This had helped to develop much good practice in departments, but this was not disseminated effectively more widely across the school.

The quarter of teachers who had experienced classroom-based action research felt positive about it. The CPD leader was keen to encourage its wider use and for it to become an important part of the school's culture because it would encourage ongoing professional dialogue before, during and after research experiences. The school had worked towards becoming self-evaluative; it now wanted to be 'research engaged'.

Aims

The aim of the initial *Effective Practices in CPD* project was to develop the opportunities for 16 second-year teachers through an Early Professional Development programme. Each term had a specific focus:

Term 1: Paired collaboration on lesson planning across departments, with a shared aim to teach Ofsted grade 2 (good) lessons.

Term 2: Work scrutiny whereby teachers were invited to collect information on a particular issue of interest through observations, questionnaires, interviews, etc.

Term 3: Small-scale action research where teachers chose a focus, conducted a very small piece of action research and presented findings at the celebration event at the end of term.

Impact of phase 1

Overall the project was very successful with full participation and engagement from the 16 second-year teachers at each stage:

- The first term's work was welcomed as teachers had an opportunity to focus on their own classroom practice as well as working across departments – a rare opportunity at the school. This enabled other benefits such as sharing good practice from one department to another.

- The structure of the second term's activities enabled teachers to begin to unpick issues they had come across in their own lessons. Ideas included 'Why do boys dominate discussions in BTEC Business?' and 'Why don't Year 8 do homework?' The collaborative approach to the investigations led to real professional dialogue and some enquiry.
- The third term's action research, although on a very small scale, engaged teachers in unpicking their own practice. The enquiries, implementation of an idea and subsequent evaluations began to encourage teachers to become more risk taking and enquiry oriented.

Staff made clear learning gains from their peer observations and were able to add value to their own teaching. This fitted in with the school's improvement plans. Their action research increased the involvement of students, who shared their views. The celebration event gave teachers a date by which they needed to complete their work, and raised their status with each other and across the school. It left the second-year teachers and their mentors wanting more – and made the project leader more convinced that all the teaching staff would benefit from even more structured enquiry and research taking place in the school. Research engagement was beginning to take off!

Phase 2 project

The next phase of the project aimed to embed and extend the achievements of phase 1 through engaging more staff in practitioner enquiry and action research. It was ambitious: now *all* teachers in their third year and beyond – about 60 teachers in total – were to work in 'action learning sets' (ALS).

Aims

The aims were to:

- embed the notion that this is a 'learning-centred' school
- engage all members of the teaching community in learning in small groups
- ensure that all teachers have a 'learning target' in their performance management (PM), linked to the action learning; recording a lesson which would show their progress
- provide opportunities for staff growth
- continue to raise standards of learning and teaching.

These aims would have benefited from being more tangible and focused on specific outcomes, including some related to pupil learning. It also seems an omission that there was no explicit aim about wanting to be a research-engaged school: the school was already learning centred and the new challenge was the action research or practitioner enquiry element.

The plan was that a small group of up to eight professionals with a shared interest in an aspect of teaching and learning would form an ALS. Each group would be facilitated by a 'learning leader'. The group would discuss the aspect they were focused on, try out a few things in the classroom, reflect and feed back. The learning leader would then add some theory such as reading an article by a leading light on the topic and share some practice or case studies carried out elsewhere. At the end of the experience, new ideas, proposals and policies would be put forward or further research carried out. Essentially the plan provided an opportunity for high-quality professional development, led by staff, for staff based in classrooms to improve the quality of teaching and learning for students.

In lieu of three professional development days (thus giving them three extra days' holiday), all teachers (except trainees, newly qualified teachers and those in their second year who had their own activities) were expected to participate in two action learning sets a year. Thus, participation was not voluntary. Each ALS was a six-week programme comprising four Thursday twilight sessions lasting between 60 and 90 minutes, with an expectation of about three hours of action research and reflection (see Table 3.1). The sessions were held at the end of the school day.

Table 3.1: Structure of ALS sessions

Session 1: 1hr	Session 2: 1hr	Session 3: 1.5hr	Session 4: 1.5hr
Socialisation	*Externalisation*	*Combination*	*Internalisation*
A 'catalyst' – discuss something that you think is happening.	If something is 'found' or said to be 'true', it gets written down.	Find others (e.g. literature/theory) to 'back up' what you say.	Possible change to practice, e.g. new strategies/policies.
	2 weeks action research	1 week reading	

The action learning sets focused on 20 interesting topics, such as:

Promoting the learning mind set

Solving the problems of the 'I can't do it' student. The aim of this ALS was to develop strategies to create learning mindsets, which would improve the behaviour, motivation and academic success of students.

Body language

The sessions looked at practical ways of uncovering habitual or unknown trends in teachers' personal body language that can either be harnessed or adapted to make sure classroom behaviour and student engagement is maximised.

Partnership teaching

Thinking of ways to embed the practice of students teaching each other in the classroom.

Mobile phones as a learning tool

All students have mobile phones. Currently they are banned, but shouldn't this technology be embraced?

Surprising students out of the classroom

Exploring 'thinking outside the box' and presenting core concepts in unusual and thought-provoking ways.

Teachers could choose which half-term during the year they would do their action learning in, as seen in Table 3.2.

Each set was led by a 'learning leader'. Eighteen teachers offered to take on this role. They had a range of experience (from between three to 30 years) but they all had a passion for and an interest in the topics which they offered. An external consultant worked with the learning leaders on establishing professional learning communities and coaching. The project director trained them in the ALS process as a group for two hours and as individuals for about 20 minutes. This was the structure of the four ALS sessions:

Socialisation

- Begin by explaining the principles of the ALS and its main theme.
- Examine the reasons why people are attending your session.
- Brainstorm what the theme means to individuals. Ask for examples of practice that teachers already have.
- Discuss why the theme of your ALS is important in education and in your school.

Table 3.2: When action learning sets were to run

Autumn 2	Spring 1	Spring 2	Summer 1
Promoting the learning mind set	Pupil voice	Dilemma-based learning	Accelerated learning
Body language	Emotional intelligence	Learning styles	Learning styles
SEAL (Social and emotional aspects of learning)	SEAL	Surprising students out of the classroom	Making use of mark schemes and examiners' reports in teaching
Vertical tutoring	Enterprising learners	Partnership teaching	(and some later additions)
Partnership teaching	Using MLE in the classroom	Accelerated learning	
	Mobile phones as a learning tool	Linking specialisms to teaching and learning	
	Five principles that underpin Fresh Start delivery	Strategies for effective teaching	

- Ask teachers to consider what they would like to have achieved at the end of the four sessions and what sorts of things they might do over four sessions.

Task: teachers to consider what they will do in their classrooms for the two-week action research.

Externalisation
- Discuss outcomes of the socialisation session, i.e. what they thought about.
- Each teacher to explain the small-scale action research they will be carrying out over a two-week period and what they would expect to find.
- Ask them to make a basic action plan – action/impact/evaluation – and share in pairs.

- Ask if they need any support.
- End with each person making a hypothesis linked to the ALS theme.

Task: teachers to carry out the two-week research.

Combination

- Share some literature/theory. This could include a clip from Teachers TV, an article, a paper, an extract from a book, research findings or case studies from elsewhere. This is an opportunity for you to supplement what your group thinks or believes to be true with some real evidence. This supports your CPD as well as theirs.
- Enable a discussion about what you have produced. Discuss initial thoughts and findings from action research.

Internalisation

- Each teacher to present their findings. Are there any overall lessons or conclusions? Do they need to review or change practice? Are there any proposals?
- Discuss what's next for individuals.

Impact of phase 2

By the end of March 2009 the project director felt that the project had only been partly successful and that it was too early to be certain of its impact (although the TDA funding was due to end in March, the project was due to run until the end of the school year). The development sessions for the learning leaders had gone well and these 18 people felt they had learned a great deal. However, they were also aware of how much more they needed to know and do. Some sets had been more successful than others and some participants had put more into them and gained more from the experience than others. Overall, there was clear evidence that most of the teachers involved had:

- attended an action learning set
- read materials (theory and research) they wouldn't have otherwise
- mixed with teachers they didn't normally speak with, from different subject areas
- discussed issues
- linked theory to their own practice in the classroom
- thought more deeply about what they do and why – as one teacher said, 'The best thing about them is that they create reflection'

- been innovative – they tried out new strategies and learned from the experience.

The extract below from notes made from an ALS discussion on principles of effective teaching (see Boxes 1 and 2) illustrates all these points. However, the reading chosen by the learning leader was rather dated and intended for university teaching. There are many, more appropriate works that might have stimulated greater thinking. This raises issues about the learning leaders' knowledge base.

Box 1: ALS – Strategies for effective teaching

Summary of discussion after reading an article about principles for good practice
- 'A' identified *frequent student–instructor contact in and out of classes* as an aspect of effective teaching, especially in relation to her Year 10s who are challenging to teach but would clearly benefit from this level of attention and interest. B felt her Year 10s could benefit from this as well.
- Group discussed the possibility of making this happen within their context.
- All agreed that time presented the most significant issue.
- All could identify groups where they felt this kind of intervention would have a positive impact on the effectiveness of the teaching and learning process.
- 'C' identified *learning is not a spectator sport* as an important issue for effectiveness and 'M' mentioned the need for teachers to stop talking and start listening.
- There was further discussion about reflective time and thinking time. 'A' suggested making use of a 'thinking group' – people who you could email with your difficulties who would reflect objectively. This needed to be investigated further and could be the basis for a further ALS.
- The constraints were discussed and a plan agreed.

Box 2: Outcomes of discussion

> The teachers decided 'to make time for student–teacher contact away from the classroom in order to better impact on effective teaching' over the following fortnight. Specifically, they agreed to:
>
> - make use of support staff to facilitate 10-minute interviews with a small number of students about coursework and how they're getting on
> - make appointments with students away from class time and monitor uptake and effectiveness
> - do research on work done so far to identify key areas of success and/or development
> - develop 'prompt' questions
> - make the interview balance 60:40 student talk:teacher talk
> - keep a learning journal
> - create an appropriate student voice to monitor impact.

As a result of another action learning set on partnership teaching, one teacher tried something innovative: asking one Year 7 class to teach another. Her reflection on this can be seen in Box 3.

Box 3: Action research by a Science teacher

> ALS: Partnership teaching
>
> *Activity*
>
> My Year 7 top set had to work in groups to research an energy resource, find out how it works, the pros and cons of using it and then teach another Year 7 class (bottom set) about it.
>
> *What were you trying to achieve?*
>
> I chose the top set so that we could push the gifted and talented pupils: some pupils would do in-depth research into things like nuclear physics which they would not usually encounter at KS3 level. I also required pupils to take some responsibility for their own learning and teach themselves about their chosen topic. Lastly, I hoped to develop the pupils' confidence and give them experience of speaking in public.

What happened?

Pupils researched their topic and prepared resources for the class that they intended to teach. We had two lessons when they practised teaching the topics to their own class and their peers provided constructive feedback and suggestions for improvement. I graded them on their posters, the materials and resources they had created and the quality of their presentation. All of the pupils worked extremely hard on their projects: most did extra work at home and developed fantastic resources. What was even better is that most of the pupils did all of the research on their own: all I had to do was steer them in the right direction on where to find the best resources. They accessed a huge range of resources, from things on the internet to A-level and GCSE textbooks, so that they could learn as much as they could about their energy resource.

The presentation day was very stressful for the pupils and especially me because they took turns to teach a bottom set Year 7 class who were renowned for poor behaviour and extremely short attention spans. Fortunately, the presentation day went off without any hitches. This activity really did stretch the pupils who gave the presentations – unfortunately, most of it went over the heads of the class being taught.

What would you change and why?

It could have been better if the 'teachers' were teaching this lesson to a class of higher ability pupils, possibly an older year group. Overall it was a very positive experience for the pupils who enjoyed the freedom that this task provided for them.

Overall judgement on the project's success

This was an ambitious project aimed at moving a whole school further down the road of becoming engaged in practitioner enquiry and being a more learning-centred and research-engaged community. As ambitious projects often are, it was only partly successful. About one-sixth of teachers did not do what they had agreed to do within the ALS or did not turn up to sessions that they had opted for. For instance, only one out of six teachers turned up to a session on body language that another staff member had put much effort into preparing. To encourage attendance, the project manager made announcements over the tannoy system on Thursdays after school to remind people that the action learning sets were due to start.

Features of effective professional development

In considering features of effective professional development, the following were definitely in place:

- specifying a focus and goal for CPD activity, aligned to clear timescales
- including a focus on pupil outcomes in CPD activity
- engaging with a variety of CPD opportunities
- including time for reflection and feedback
- ensuring collaborative approaches to CPD
- developing strategic leadership of CPD.

However, the following were not sufficiently in place:

- Establishing clarity of purpose at the outset in CPD activity

The project director was not entirely clear on the purpose, sometimes settling for 'I just want people to talk more' rather than doing action research. Learning leaders varied in how clear they were, but participants were not entirely clear about what was meant to be achieved through the action learning sets.

- Understanding how to evaluate the impact of CPD

Although the project director knew how to evaluate impact, the project would have been strengthened by a clearer baseline picture and a greater focus on the intended impact of the project – and what evidence would be used to judge it. The successes and challenges in evaluating the impact of CPD needed earlier consideration; by the end of March no decisions had been made on how to evaluate the project. The project director was planning to meet with a group of learning leaders to decide on success criteria, but this should have been decided at the outset in order to ensure clarity.

- Ensuring participants' ownership of CPD activity

The compulsory nature of this project meant that not all teachers felt ownership. More needed to be done to win the hearts and minds of the more experienced teachers to this way of working. The compulsory status of the ALS seemed counter-productive to the ethos of learning-centred communities.

Overall, these points would have benefited from further consideration:

- More structured procedures: the project would have benefited from reminders, chasing, getting people to commit to turning up and then doing some action research in the classroom. Early career teachers had been socialised to be responsible and did not need to be chivvied, but it appeared that other teachers needed tighter systems of accountability.
- Common recording systems: ALS leaders made up their own recording systems so these varied from the purely verbal to the over-detailed. Although the project director did not want to be prescriptive, a common paper trail or reporting format would have saved time.
- The value of a specific focus and goal for CPD activity aligned to clear timescales: although these were in place, the timescales of each action learning set were short. Having a longer timescale for each ALS might have resulted in more being achieved. The timescale for the whole ALS – four one- or one-and-a-half-hour sessions over six weeks – was very short, bearing in mind how busy the teachers were.
- Time: making use of development days would have improved the quality of the time given to the ALS rather than holding the sessions after school when people were tired and felt they wanted to do other, more pressing, work or go home.
- Colleagues teaching colleagues: although this had its positive aspects, more could have been done to ensure that learning leaders had strong knowledge of the latest thinking within their topics so that they shared the best and most appropriate theory and research with their action learning sets.
- Realistic targets: the project was over-ambitious in involving all teachers in the time frame.
- Inclusivity: the ALS only involved teachers, but many support staff would have benefited from and contributed to the sets. This seemed a missed opportunity to integrate systems for support staff and teachers.

Chapter 4

The impact of extended provision

John Tandy

Context

This project involved a network of six primary schools in challenging circumstances which work cooperatively on a range of issues for the benefit of all pupils. It is based in two neighbouring local authorities (LAs). The network was established in 2002, and initially the (then) National College for School Leadership (NCSL) provided some support in running and managing the network. The schools work together on projects in which they share an interest, and there is an opt-out if a project is not appropriate for an individual school. Projects have included joint research, learning walks, joint workshops and working parties.

All network schools took part in the *Effective Practices in CPD* project and were represented by approximately 10 per cent of teaching and support staff, some of whom work in the extended services and some as teaching assistants. This was a carefully structured and planned project that succeeded in bringing teaching and support staff together to address a common aspect of their work and develop their awareness of its effectiveness to inform future thinking.

Phase 1 project

At the beginning of the project the network had successfully experienced collaborative working. CPD activities tended to be planned by the group of headteachers in a variety of ways, including meetings and via telephone conversations. Although a great deal of success had been achieved, this way of working had sometimes led to schools compromising on objectives in order to reach agreement more easily and quickly. The design of projects and the participation of a school could depend on who was present at meetings. Compromise was more the result of the headteachers' workload than of a lack of commitment to the work of the network. The emphasis had been on learning for teaching staff, and development for support staff had been a lower priority. Support staff were employed to work during session times and had not had opportunities to engage in CPD activity as part of their paid hours.

Aim

The main aim of the project was to evaluate the impact of aspects of extended schools provision in the network, while at the same time developing and enhancing the skills and self-awareness of relevant staff. All of the schools in the network were very aware that, although they were collectively offering a wide range of extended services in the belief that these would add additional value to the work of their various establishments, there was very little systematic evaluation of the impact of these activities, nor were there mechanisms to link pupil progress and pupil needs to what extended provision had to offer. Extended provision was felt to be 'a good thing' but this could not be quantified. There were no explicit concerns about the quality of provision, but it was felt that it would be useful for people to use the opportunities provided by the network to work together with colleagues from schools in similar areas.

In phase 1 of the project the schools appointed a project coordinator, who had previously worked at one of the primary schools in the network, to work in a consultancy role. Her first task was to carry out a systematic audit of the aims of the individual schools and of their available areas of expertise. She worked with each headteacher in the network to ascertain their aspirations for the project, determine the needs of the individual school and, eventually, to propose a project design that would be appropriate and relevant to all participating schools. She also suggested ways of using existing expertise to develop colleagues' potential. The proposed design of the project was agreed by schools. The headteachers of the network schools selected which aspects of their extended services were to be evaluated.

The second process that was set up was a mechanism to train staff who were to lead evaluation in their school. Within the group of schools there were middle managers who had completed some action research and were competent at handling data on performance and effectiveness. This group worked together with the consultant to develop their understanding of how extended services could be evaluated. Development workers from the LAs' extended services department were also included in this group as they have a wide reach and knowledge. They decided to use a range of measures and processes to evaluate impact, for example:

- observations
- well-being scaling
- approaches suitable for use with young children, e.g. drawing themselves in variety of situations
- pupil questionnaires
- pupil interviews and discussions.

(See Appendix for examples of evaluating extended school activity)

Once participants had been trained, they worked in their respective schools with support staff, through coaching, to lead the evaluation. They worked together to agree appropriate ways of evaluating the impact of services in order to support improvements in delivery that would, in turn, facilitate the gathering of important data on the effectiveness of activities for groups and individual pupils. The project also provided opportunities to extend leadership, as the middle managers involved had to direct the work of a small team: for most of the teachers, this was the first time they had worked as coaches with support staff. Loosely, the aim was to encourage support staff to reflect on and consolidate their learning. It was also regarded as a way of enabling participants to link the aims of their school with how their personal practice contributed to those aims. The headteachers wanted to use this work to give the teachers an opportunity to lead and to manage a project in their home school, something that otherwise may not have been available to them.

Each school identified two aspects of practice to provide a focus for the project and to ensure manageability. The headteachers agreed with the consultant who led the training that the focus would first be on qualitative – and later on quantitative – measures, and reflect their priorities of pupils' well-being and attitudes.

The lead teacher in each school developed the action plan with the support staff team. Each plan included a strict time line, and was to be implemented by teachers and support staff in each school.

Funding for the project enabled the participating support staff to be paid for the time they spent on CPD activities. This enhanced existing goodwill, 'oiled the wheels' and helped to ensure that the project progressed. There was already goodwill from support staff, but it was felt that they were entitled to be paid for the additional time they spent working on the project. Lack of funding had previously impeded their involvement in similar CPD activities.

Following the training, participants had to complete a pilot 'mini' evaluation task in school and then meet again with the training group to share findings and compare notes. Participants drew up an action plan to complete the evaluation. Each headteacher oversaw and monitored the project in their own school and ensured that milestones were being met as it progressed. In turn the headteachers shared outcomes at network meetings.

The first year of the project went well. It was felt that having a consultant to manage the project was important, as she had the capacity to ensure that the project was designed to be appropriate for all participating schools, to deliver the training and to monitor and evaluate the success of the project.

The training sessions were complemented by opportunities for participants with common areas of work in network schools to discuss and to share aspects of their practice and to learn from each others' experience and ideas. This was felt to be important since there had been little or no CPD opportunities, for example, to manage an effective breakfast club. Working practice evolved by drawing on the collective ideas of people in the respective schools. Support staff stated that it:

- gave them practical ideas
- allowed them to find out about systems in use in other schools
- gave them quality time with their extended school service colleagues.

Phase 2 project

Evaluation feedback sheets collated from the first phase of the project were used to establish how continuation could usefully progress. Headteachers' planning meetings confirmed the value of phase 1 work: some headteachers requested that additional (or alternative) staff were included in the continuation group. One headteacher who had originally been reluctant to commit fully to the project was very willing to commit to phase 2.

Many of the staff who participated in the second phase of the project had also taken part in phase 1. The majority of participants felt that the CPD had been productive and wanted time to consolidate their learning, work with colleagues and share good practice further.

Schools were again able to work with some of the initial participants to develop their skills and also to use their expertise and experience to have a positive impact on those members of staff who formed the basis of the continuation group.

The headteachers of the participating schools felt this was a good opportunity to extend similar learning to additional staff at both teacher and support staff level. Many of the support staff had had very few opportunities for development or networking with other colleagues carrying out similar roles. There were also further opportunities to develop middle leadership for some staff who were at an early stage of their career.

Discussion at headteachers' planning meetings indicated that the National Occupational and Professional Standards for supporting teaching and learning in schools were new to each school. Headteachers agreed that this project would be an ideal opportunity to introduce them to staff and to get feedback.

All staff involved in the project were introduced to the new National Standards for staff supporting teaching and learning in schools, in particular those that related to extra-curricular activities. Using these Standards reinforced the important role of extended school activities in delivering outcomes. The possibility for using these standards for performance management in some schools was also explored.

A consultant was again employed to negotiate and to liaise with both headteachers and with staff teams, who now had the confidence to suggest ways of working on the focus and approaches for phase 2.

Impact of the projects

Examples of the impact of phase 1 and 2 projects are shown in Tables 4.1 and 4.2.

Table 4.1: Examples of projects and outcomes: Phase 1

School	Extended provision focus	Evaluation outcomes	Impact of evaluation
School 1	Maths club	Attendance at Maths club leads to enhanced self-image in Maths.	Children targeted to join Maths club.
School 2	Breakfast club	Older children play with younger children, social skills are enhanced. Pupils enjoy coming to the club: many choose to attend. Children identify preferred activities.	Provision of additional play materials for which children express and demonstrate preference.
School 3	Reading club	Evaluation showed that pupils developed an enjoyment of reading and read at home, sometimes to a sibling.	Pupils targeted to join Reading club.
School 4	ICT club	Use of ICT at club leads to improved completion rates of homework; use of available learning software supports enhanced development of literacy and numeracy skills.	Pupils with poor homework completion targeted to join club. Additional learning software purchased to enhance opportunities to develop literacy and numeracy skills.

Maths club

Initial evaluation results indicated that children who attended the club were not positive about Maths lessons. After eight weeks, evaluation of the children who attended the Maths club showed that they had an enhanced self-image in Maths. Evaluation was done by asking the children to draw a simple picture of themselves outside and then attending Maths club. This was done at the beginning of their attendance and eight weeks later. The number of smiley faces attending Maths club increased by the end of the eight-week period. As a result of this positive result, the school decided to identify and target children who it was felt would benefit from attending the Maths club. The children's progress is being tracked on an ongoing basis as a follow-up to this first phase of evaluation.

Breakfast club

Analysis of attendance at the Breakfast club showed that those children who attended chose to attend, i.e. they were not obliged to because of home circumstances. Observations noted that older children played with younger children, something that never happened in mainstream school. It was observed that the social skills of children who attended the club were enhanced.

> *The well ordered, organised and good quality breakfast and after-school club are assets to the school and of benefit to pupils.*
>
> (Ofsted, 2009)

Reading club

Attitudes to reading were researched by interviewing pupils on an ongoing basis to track their feelings about Reading club activities and whether they were enjoying reading. A questionnaire was given to parents and/or carers to invite their perceptions of impact. The findings surprised staff who found out that children spent a lot of time reading at home and that they also read aloud to siblings and to favourite toys, imitating some aspects of story time practice at the club. This resulted in identifying pupils who would benefit and encouraging them to join the club in order to promote positive attitudes to reading.

ICT club

The ICT club gave children an opportunity to use computers in order to practise their skills and to enjoy using ICT. Children were able to use ICT facilities to complete their homework (e.g. using Word and the internet) or to use curriculum-related software (e.g. Espresso). The research findings were that children chose to use the opportunities to work on their homework and that the completion rates of homework increased among children who attended. Literacy skills were also enhanced as the children used words and text in the software.

Staff outcomes

Members of support staff who took part in training developed a greater understanding of how they contributed to the work of the extended services of the school and how extended provision complemented the work of the official school day and contributed to the overall success of the school. They stated that they 'feel more important and see what they do matters', that '[after-school clubs] are not just there for child minding' and that 'it gave them [a] chance to say what they thought they could do'. This was an important part of the training. One teacher moved on to the NCSL's Leadership Pathways training. The lead teacher in another primary school was given responsibility for the performance review of support staff.

The following is an example of the impact on an individual pupil, tracked during phase 1 of the project (although, of course, it is difficult to know how much was due specifically to their involvement in the project):

> Pupil A joined the Eco Club and Playground Buddies club in her school during Year 6 (phase 1). She had special educational needs (SEN) and had been a loner and had been underachieving. At the end of Year 6 she achieved Level 3b in reading and writing, above her Fischer Family Trust (FFT) target of 3.2; level 4c in Maths (FFT 2.6) and level 4c (FFT 3.4) in science. She was voted Citizen of the Year by her peers at the end of Year 6.

Work with the National Occupational and Professional Standards was abandoned in the context of the projects. It had been thought that the Standards relating to out-of-school provision would inform expectations of ways in which support staff should be working. However, it was quickly recognised that the support staff involved in the project were working at a level that was higher than the relevant standard on the Standards framework. They were therefore not felt to be appropriate to guide the work of support staff in the extended provision and were not used. They were, however, retained to inform performance review processes.

Schools did not yet feel in a position to attribute improvements in pupil attainment exclusively to the work of extra-curricular provision as it tended to complement curriculum provision. However, pupil outcomes were tracked and progress will be analysed at the end of the academic year of phase 2. Early indicators are positive.

Table 4.2: Examples of projects and outcomes: Phase 2

Name of school	Extended school activity	Nature of focus	Measurement being used	Links with school targets	Evaluation outcome
School 1	Developing a newspaper (KS2)	Boys' writing skills	Pre- and post-attitudinal survey and writing sample analysis	Boys' writing is a whole-school target	Pupils were willing to contribute to purposeful and functional writing. Improved attitudes identified during course of project. Quality of writing improved during project.
School 2	Reading club (KS1 and 2)	Pupil attitudes to reading	Pre- and post-reading ages and change in pupil attitude survey	Reading is a basic skill and always a whole-school target	Incremental improvement in reading ages. Improved attitudes to reading.
School 3	ICT club linked to international work (KS2)	Pupil attitudes to other communities and cultures	Pupil attitudinal survey and pre- and post-ICT skill analysis as an outcome from club	Links with community cohesion and gaining of ICT skill, both whole-school targets	Impact mostly neutral. No negative feedback but attitudes largely unchanged. ICT skills enhanced.
School 4	Mathsletics activity (software package) (KS2)	Increased Maths ability	Pre- and post-analysis of pupil Maths expertise	Maths is a basic skill and always a whole-school target area	Incremental development and improvement in Maths expertise.

Overall judgement on the project's success

The project was clearly a success. It enabled the component institutions in the network to evaluate the impact of aspects of their extended provision and succeeded in enhancing the professional knowledge, skills and understanding as well as the confidence of staff who engaged with the projects. Support staff were now taking a more proactive role than before; for example, they put forward children for whom an aspect of provision would be appropriate given their levels of progress. Headteachers said that they plan and manage activities with the lead teacher with a confidence that they did not previously have.

Although network schools were pleased with the outcomes of the project and it was felt that the action plans and their delivery were satisfactory, the chosen model would have been even better if the headteachers had been more actively involved in monitoring the delivery of the action plan, and in a position not only to support but also advise participants.

Working as a network enabled schools to benefit from bespoke development that was designed to meet their needs, something that would not normally be available: project funding enabled this to be put in place. The headteachers affirmed the importance of being able to bounce ideas off one another and to draw on their collective wisdom when formulating the aims of the project, without being constrained by having to coordinate the work of the project themselves. The additional capacity provided by the consultant was valued. The sharing of good practice was enriched by being able to draw on a broad range of practice.

The aims of the project were very clearly set out and were part of an existing planned project which already had the commitment of the leaders involved. At the end of the project they had achieved what they had set out to do. The feedback was very clear about how much participants had learned from each other. The project had an impact on the children's learning as well as on the participants, whose skills were developed in a number of ways (as outlined above). What was learned was embedded in practice.

Previous CPD practice in the network had often meant using 'best fit' external courses to address needs, assuming they were available: often they were not specifically about extended services. The impact of CPD had been variable. The project funding enabled schools to work in a way appropriate to their needs.

Features of effective professional development

To summarise, and in considering the features of effective professional development, the following were in place to a varying degree:

- establishing clarity of purpose at the outset in CPD activity
- specifying a focus and goal for CPD activity, aligned to clear timescales
- including a focus on pupil outcomes in CPD activity
- ensuring participants' ownership of CPD activity
- engaging with a variety of CPD opportunities
- including time for reflection and feedback
- ensuring collaborative approaches to CPD.

These were in place to a lesser degree:

- understanding how to evaluate the impact of CPD
- developing strategic leadership of CPD.

The project would have been more successful had a concrete evidence base for expected impact on pupils' learning and well-being been established and this impact tracked more rigorously. Although there had been an initial emphasis on qualitative measures with plans for the use of quantitative measures at a later stage, it is likely that further success would have been possible if there had been greater clarity about the measurable learning gains children had achieved from the outset. This would have enabled these improvements to be identified and monitored as well as the ways in which provision contributed to pupils' wellbeing and attitudes, since the two aspects are closely linked.

Appendix

Examples of approaches to evaluation of an extended school activity

Method 1

This was based on evaluating the impact upon pupils of an after-school cookery club. The following would be tracked for the pupils attending the club:

- Use TDA scales re behaviour, attitude, self-confidence, improved relations, raised aspirations
- Monitor pupils' eating habits and whether they improve
- Observe pupils' mood on going home, i.e. at the end of club
- Give questionnaires to pupils before and after club asking them to complete statements such as 'What I enjoyed most at cookery club is…' Use pictures of tools with statements, e.g. 'I can use…'
- Observe pupils during the club, i.e. on their acquisition of skills in chopping, cutting, grating, etc. (also teamwork, cooperation, etc.).

Method 2

- Use questionnaires to ascertain what pupils like about the club
- Identify which aspects of the club satisfy the outcomes of ECM before the evaluation so it is outcome specific
- Use breakfast club (for example) to build in an activity to support, for example, vulnerable children and fulfil their needs
- Identify cohort who are attending the club: is there a specific group attending, e.g. gifted and talented, SEN, under-achieving boys?

OR

- Identify the group first and then target the club to raise their attainment/attitude/attendance/behaviour, etc. (In this way the evaluation is easily undertaken because the pre-assessment has been done by identifying the group and post-activity evaluation can be a repeat of this.)

Enjoyment – how to measure whether this is happening?

- Question children about what they want
- What worked well?
- Photographic evidence
- See who attends – can they be categorised?
- Friendships – do children make different friends when at a club?
- Does it impact upon school attendance?
- How involved are the children; track one child in the morning
- Involve clubs in the life of the school, e.g. breakfast club input in assembly, star of the week, report back to school on what is happening in the clubs
- Display board in school to publicise activities and pupils' comments to support this.

Parents' views – seek their opinion on whether a club has had an impact upon their son/daughter in any way.

Chapter 5

Coaching to improve teaching and learning and to develop leadership capacity

Vivienne Porritt

Context

The school involved in this project is a larger-than-average secondary school which has mathematics and computing specialist status. The socio-economic profile of the area the school serves is favourable, with some parts experiencing social disadvantage. The proportion of students who are eligible for free school meals or who have learning difficulties and/or disabilities is well below average. The school has a strong record in improving the quality of its teaching and learning and saw involvement in the *Effective Practices in CPD* project as a way to develop this further.

Phase 1 project

The school has worked for three years to establish a consistent teaching methodology. New teachers took little time to settle into the school as there was such a clearly established way of working. External CPD opportunities were of a variable quality and the expertise in school was not effectively utilised. Teachers felt that CPD was about external opportunities and often its impact was limited to the teacher who had accessed the CPD opportunity, which was evaluated through feedback forms immediately on completion. Support staff also engaged in CPD activity. The school found the impact of the expenditure difficult to evaluate, and traditional methods of evaluation lacked depth, detail and genuine reflection. Cascading the learning from external CPD was often an issue, with some teachers lacking either the time or the confidence to share what they had learned. There was no culture of sharing between colleagues and when this did happen it was often confined to departments and subject content took precedence over pedagogy. There was also a need for greater consistency to ensure that the percentage of good or better lessons continued to increase.

The school was open to developing coaching: one of the senior leadership team had introduced eight coaches who had learned relevant skills and worked with individual teachers on a one-to-one basis. Some of the participants felt threatened by their involvement and had been 'scarred by bad memories of coaching'. Coaching was not seen as a high-status activity and was not being used to bring about improvements where under-performance was noted.

Aims

The aims of the first phase of the project were to:

- re-establish coaching as an effective CPD opportunity in the school
- support a consistent use of the school's agreed pedagogical approach
- support new teachers in using the school's pedagogical approach
- bring about specific improvements where the under-performance of some teachers was noted.

The appointment of a new deputy head with experience of coaching trios, combined with the application for *Effective Practices in CPD* project funding, offered a chance to develop a different approach to coaching. Senior leadership, analysis of the previous, less successful coaching experience identified that this CPD activity had two competing aims. These were a desire to embed the school's approach to teaching and learning, and the need to tackle under-performance. This lack of clarity over the specific focus and outcome for the CPD activity led to confusion and concern over its purpose among participants. There were 16 new staff at the school and there was a pressing need to ensure that they were able to work within the school's approach to teaching and learning.

The process adopted was that of coaching trios. Each trio consisted of a coach, a volunteer who had expressed interest and a teacher who was new to the school. In some cases, the 'volunteer' had been targeted and strongly encouraged to participate due to needs identified through performance management discussions. Eight people who had previously worked as coaches were assigned two trios each, across an academic year. The eight coaches had varying roles across the school, and were selected for their potential skills rather than because they held posts of responsibility. Coaches and the colleagues they worked with were carefully matched by leadership team members. The group of coaches met each half-term to share good practice and to develop ideas. The coaching process was then linked to the core dimensions of the Teacher Learning Academy (TLA) to further support reflective discussion and thinking by individuals and within the trios.

The coaching model was adapted from the widely used GROW model[1] that had been introduced to the school prior to its involvement in the *Effective Practices in CPD* project. Clear principles and processes were put in place, including the following:

- An initial meeting was held to introduce ground rules, establish the focus and timescale of the project.
- The project's focus was agreed between the three participants, with support from a participant's head of department in some cases.
- All three participants agreed to explore the same focus and to plan lessons together, to observe and feed back to each other.

Observation of lessons provided the central focus of development. Successful teaching and learning strategies were co-constructed and modelled by each individual. With the support of the coach, teachers determined the focus for learning, based on their analysis of their own practice. The learning was evaluated via a TLA submission.

Impact of phase 1

By the end of the first phase of the project, the school had a well-established approach to coaching. Fourteen trios had completed a coaching cycle. Eight coaches had received TLA Stage 1 recognition for their work and 12 participants used their coaching trio as the focus of a TLA submission at either Stage 1 or Stage 2. This process encouraged participants to reflect more clearly on the application of the coaching discussions to the classroom. Coaching was accorded a central role in the creation of a professional learning community, which was one of the key priorities in the new school development plan (2008–11).

The project leader evaluated the impact of the coaching trios, using the following evidence sources:

- TLA submissions
- lesson observation gradings
- formal feedback via evaluation sheets
- minutes from coaching meetings.

Feedback by participants about the process was positive. Of the 21 responses received, all teachers reported that the process had helped them to improve their practice; three new teachers felt it was a great opportunity to meet staff

---

[1] G = Goal (for the session and/or project); R = Reality (the current state of play); O = Options (possible ways forward); W = Will (level of commitment to the planned action).

from other departments to see how they worked; seven felt the process was invaluable in enabling them to embed new ways of working such as 'learning to learn'. All but one of the participants were willing to be involved again and all reported an impact upon their classroom practice. Teachers reported that they could focus on their areas for development in a 'risk-free' environment and that the feedback was more helpful than in formal observations. Specific areas of improved practice were reported to include higher expectations and good behaviour. Teachers were able to see how students worked in other areas of the curriculum, thus supporting greater consistency. New teachers felt 'part of the teaching community' as a result of their work and that the experience was 'friendly, supportive and positive'. Overall, participants reported an improvement in their own professional practice and an increased sense of belonging to a professional learning community.

The project leader felt that teaching teams within the school benefited from the new ideas gleaned from members of other teams. This was also enhanced by TLA submissions as the requirement to share learning with other colleagues perhaps stimulated more systematic sharing of practice than before.

For coaches, the year yielded professional benefits: three were promoted during the year, and further promotions have since taken place. Individuals learned when coaching was appropriate and when it was not. One coach had experience of helping to identify the issues lying beneath under-performance and then enabling other processes to support the further development of an individual teacher. Another coach said the skills developed helped her to 'see the wood for the trees and so reduce the snowball of problems being identified'. She felt this experience was instrumental in gaining a leadership post in the school. Although this cannot be directly attributable to their development and experience as a coach, the project leader stated the leadership team had seen 'the sense of professional confidence from each individual blossom'.

For the school, the approach to coaching provided more stability in a year that, because of staffing changes, might otherwise have been turbulent. The fear that the school's approach to teaching might be lost proved unfounded as new teachers were given opportunities to put into practice the ideas explored through working with experienced practitioners.

The school's internal lesson observations showed that the school's pedagogical approach was well embedded and new teachers had a clear understanding of whole-school expectations which had been a key aim of phase 1. Coaching had thus been an invaluable induction process as it offered personalised learning for new teachers. The number of good or better lessons remained stable as seen by internal observation data. The school felt this was an achievement, given the significant changes to the staff profile during 2007–8 (including six teachers on maternity leave and eight newly qualified teachers). The coaching trios had also targeted some under-performing and less experienced teachers. Maintaining standards therefore suggested to the school that the coaching process had improved the quality of teaching. The percentage of inadequate lessons continued to fall (a three-year trend) and the quality of teaching in the Sixth form improved.

It is clear that the project enabled the school to develop a stronger and more reflective approach to professional learning. Coaching offered valuable additionality to the induction process of new teachers. Coaching in trios was seen as less confrontational than the one-to-one process that had previously been used, and had helped to develop informal and collegiate relationships across departments in a large organisation.

Particular factors that brought success included:

- The short timescale of three to four weeks for the trios to plan, observe and feed back among the group gave urgency to the process, gave it a specific focus and goal and spurred participants to achieve small-scale success.
- Selecting the right people as coaches.

Improvements identified by the school were that NQTs could have been involved in the coaching process earlier in the year. Due to the sheer number of staff involved, some NQTs had to wait until the summer term to participate. The school also recognised the tension between wanting to involve more staff each year in a successful process, while appreciating that it was vitally important for quality assurance and capacity reasons that the number of coaches and trios was regulated. Subsequent follow-up to the trio process was voluntary and informal, and many participants continued to support each other informally. Some participants expressed a desire for a more formal opportunity to meet again and it would be worth considering whether there is value in a subsequent formal review of whether changes in practice have been embedded, using the coaching trio.

It would also have been valuable to track more thoroughly the specific improvements in classroom practice by teachers supported by the coaching. This would offer the opportunity to evaluate the impact of improved teaching upon the quality of pupils' learning. Improvements in standards in specific classes were asserted, but the school had not seen the value in matching concrete evidence of the impact upon pupils' learning to the coaching activity.

Phase 2 project

The first phase of the project had developed a culture which offered a good platform to develop coaching as a leadership disposition.

Aim

The aim of phase 2 was to embed coaching to improve the quality of teaching and learning and develop leadership capacity.

In the second phase the school decided to use the trio approach to provide support for developing leaders among the teaching staff and to begin to develop a leadership programme for support staff. Several middle leaders were new to the school and had not experienced coaching as a development activity prior to joining the school. Volunteers were again sought from middle leaders.

Initially a member of the support staff was included in the original cohort of coaches, but this had not been successful because some teachers were not ready to collaborate with a support colleague. The school now judged the climate to be more suitable for this development.

Impact of phase 2

Formal coaching development was offered and three new coaches were inducted. Coaches worked with teachers in middle leadership positions in trios. One middle leader, new to the school, had not heard of coaching before and was invited to be involved. This colleague had a very positive experience and felt it had helped to share concerns outside of the team in which they worked. The focus for coaching had been to support the team in changing its working practices: the coaching helped the middle leader to focus more directly on the relevant issues and come to a personal solution. This colleague commented: 'We are invested in each other.' The coaching experience was seen as the high point of the induction process as opposed to more traditional approaches.

One very experienced middle leader was actively encouraged to participate. It was noted that:

> I felt everyone was doing it and they said that they had learned from it so I was curious to see what I could learn. My initial feeling was also that it would be frowned on if I didn't.

In the coaching dialogue, this colleague valued the collaborative planning which helped to focus on improving an aspect of practice. As a result of the coaching dialogue, this colleague rewrote materials and tasks to support greater differentiation. Coaching was also rated as a more effective CPD activity than any previously experienced over a long career.

In terms of leadership development, the school now feels that coaching is embedded as a practice across the group of participants. The evidence from feedback meetings suggests that the relationships have moved beyond formally scheduled coaching sessions and are working at a deeper level. Several participants now use their coach as the first point of contact when issues arise and are being supported through difficulties using the coaching model rather than being given advice. Leadership forum meeting notes and informal feedback from the leadership team suggest that when middle leaders have a personnel or performance issue to address they will use coaching techniques as a matter of course rather than a last resort. This is leading to a greater number of issues being managed at a local level rather than being referred to a member of the senior team.

The school reports increased participation among leaders at all levels in whole-school strategic leadership. A recent review of the school development plan was well attended by all middle leaders from across the school. Staff were encouraged to review and comment upon the leadership team's evaluation of progress and suggest future priorities. The confidence that emerged from this review was attributed to the power of coaching across the school. Seven trios have completed their work in this year's cycle, a wider variety of staff have been involved and participant feedback continues to be very positive.

While not fully embedding key school issues (such as learning to learn and assessment for learning), the trios gave participants the opportunity to try new techniques and take risks. This has had the effect of increasing confidence with techniques and enabling good practice to be both modelled and shared. The impact was greater in the autumn of 2008 when there was the opportunity to run a number of trios. With Year 11 and 13 pressures in spring 2009, trios had to be delayed or rearranged. Participants continue to develop TLA submissions on key themes and the trios' areas of focus. The number of good lessons observed remained constant, despite observations being targeted at areas of concern and under-performance in the school.

Trio coaching continued to be embedded across the school and moved into areas of the school where it previously had little impact. The trio way of working is now an accepted means of professional development across the school, with broad acceptance from all colleagues that they will participate in trios as part of their professional development. The school is now a TLA Centre and staff are engaging in planned, reflective CPD as part of the performance management process – and trio coaching contributes to this process. There is a drive towards developing leadership at all levels and the term 'coaching conversation' has become part of the language of leadership within the school.

Discussion with pupils showed they were aware that some of their teachers were actively trying out new teaching techniques and strategies. They experienced teachers videoing their own teacher's lesson and talking to them about their reactions to the lesson. They were also aware that the school had developed a more structured approach to starters and plenaries and that lessons were more participatory and fun. They particularly valued it when an individual teacher asked their opinion of the way the lesson had worked. As one noted:

The teachers ask us if the teaching activities are working and they would go back to the drawing board and start again if needed.

The school identified further aspects for improvement. Of the three new coaches, only one had continued in the role, which reiterates the need to select the right people. The project leader described the attributes of their effective coaches as:

- good classroom teachers
- enthusiastic
- see themselves as learners
- completer–finishers.

More colleagues are asking to be coached, so the tension between quality and increased numbers continues. The make-up of the coaching trios was also an important consideration and time needed to be devoted to this.

Work is progressing with support staff leadership, and a development programme which places coaching at its core is being planned: 14 participants from among the support staff have been identified. Further development on coaching as a leadership disposition is now planned to enable coaching to become embedded within teams as well as across teams.

The school could also consider extending its student voice work by developing selected pupils to evaluate improvements in teaching and learning strategies. There is also possible potential for coaching skills to become part of the repertoire of performance management reviewers. One participant highlighted the differences implicit in collegiate coaching to develop and improve and a hierarchical approach to performance management, and believed it was difficult to reconcile the two approaches.

Overall judgement on the project's success

This has been a very successful project in meeting its stated aims, even though the project leader considered it to be only 'successful'. She felt that the project had:

Sharpened my understanding of how to evaluate impact and so improve the CPD activity.

One comment highlighted the strong professional learning culture that has been developed:

CPD and coaching has become such an accepted part of the way we do things here.

Features of effective professional development

These features of effective professional development were in place across both project phases:

- the value of time for reflection and feedback: this was central to the coaching process
- the value of a specific focus and goal for CPD activity, aligned to clear timescales: this was a strong feature in the success of coaching trios
- participants' ownership of CPD activity: the agreed focus of the coaching showed ownership
- the significance of collaborative CPD: there was collaboration between all members of the coaching trio and this has continued informally for many
- the importance of strategic leadership of CPD: the school targeted particular people to support induction and performance and to develop consistency in teaching and learning.

These were in place to a lesser degree:

- the need for clarity of purpose at the outset in CPD activity: the purpose was explicit to the leadership team and the coaches but not always to people invited to participate
- understanding how to evaluate the impact of CPD: the evidence collected was mostly in the form of participant feedback and reactions, with lesson observation data being attributed to the impact of the coaching process.

The project would have been more successful by:

- including improved outcomes for pupils within the agreed coaching focus
- establishing a concrete evidence base for expected impact upon classroom practice and pupils' learning and tracking this impact more rigorously.

Chapter 6

Developing coaching as an effective method of CPD

Steve Illingworth

Context

This project involved secondary schools in one local authority (LA) that had used coaching on a small scale but had not seen it as an important method of development. Those teachers who were involved had told senior leaders and LA consultants that they found coaching really useful, so it was decided to extend and develop the coaching programme.

Central to this extension of coaching in the LA, developed through the *Effective Practices in CPD* project, was a more systematic and meaningful approach to evaluating its impact as a CPD activity. The project was led by the local authority's School Improvement Service which works with secondary schools, many of which are in challenging circumstances. Members of the LA secondary strategy consultant team managed the project. The aim was to enhance the work which the secondary team was doing, initially, with six 'schools causing concern' and then, later on, with other schools.

Phases 1 and 2 of the project

Teachers go away smiling.

You have one new idea to take away.

You have a chance to get ideas from other colleagues.

Comments such as these were typical of attempts at 'impact evaluation' in the LA and probably in most other parts of the country too. These comments represented the baseline and were how colleagues generally indicated that a CPD session had been successful. Although these observations were usually made with sincerity and enthusiasm, they were not very helpful when it came to evaluating the impact of CPD and deciding how much direct difference certain activities had made to learning in the classroom.

Aims

Throughout the two years that the *Effective Practices in CPD* project ran, the central aim was to develop a culture of coaching as a CPD strategy in secondary schools in the LA. A model would be produced to help evaluate the impact of CPD on both the practice of teachers and on the standards of pupil learning in the classroom. In the second phase, from 2008–9, the particular emphasis was on extending and embedding the coaching programme in secondary schools, and also on the importance of showing more clearly the impact of coaching upon everyday teaching and learning. A constant message underpinning the project was that it was about two things:

- partly about CPD to change the practice of teachers, but
- mainly about CPD which was to lead directly to improvements for pupils.

In devising a structure for the project, the impact evaluation approach offered by the London Centre for Leadership in Learning (LCLL) at the Institute of Education was used. The classification of CPD into products, processes and outcomes was used to identify the project's baseline position and the impact gained. These were used to assess impact at regular intervals: initially when considering the baseline position of the project, at interim stages and also at the end. The baseline position at the start of the project is set out below.

Products

Baseline: some secondary schools had been involved in coaching, but there was no common system or policy that could help senior leaders in schools to use coaching effectively as a means to school improvement. The evidence for this was that there was no reference to coaching in school action plans. From the LA's point of view, some secondary strategy consultants had been involved in coaching prior to September 2007, but there was no LA policy or guidance nor was there any regular commitment to coaching as part of the deployment of the consultants. This could be seen in the lack of any LA policy or guidance document or reference to coaching on consultant deployment plans. This lack of guidance meant that there was no hard evidence of the impact of coaching and no systematic way for individuals to measure the impact of their coaching.

Processes

Baseline: the development of coaching was very limited. Only five teachers from the six schools involved in the project had engaged with development sessions in the principles of coaching offered by the LA. Only one of the six schools had a group of teachers engaging in coaching on a regular basis. The evidence for these processes, or lack of them, could be seen in the records of LA consultant work and in the records of planning meetings between the local authority and senior leaders in the schools.

Outcomes/Impact

Baseline: this was measured mainly by the assessment for learning (AfL) lesson review grids (devised by the National Strategies), showing the quality of teachers' AfL practice before they benefited from coaching. These grids were completed by teacher observers, LA consultants and senior leaders during lesson observations. Where this evidence was available from the six schools, teachers' practice in aspects of AfL was recognised to be in need of further development, and was usually classed in the 'developing' stage of the AfL lesson review grid. On the pupils' section of the review grids, the achievements of pupils were often limited. In many cases this limitation was in the area of the ability of and opportunity for pupils to discuss and contribute towards the success criteria. Again, this could be seen in review grids completed in observations and also by teachers' self-analysis as they produced a baseline of the current situation in their classrooms at the start of the project.

  The main challenge faced by this project was to raise the status of coaching as an effective CPD activity in the eyes of teachers, particularly senior leaders, in schools. The recent emphasis on self-evaluation in schools has led to a culture of regular lesson observation judgements by line managers, where the focus has been more on producing accurate assessments of where teachers are in their practice and less on developing a constructive dialogue to help them to improve. Within the context of this monitoring culture, it has been a challenge to establish a CPD method such as coaching, which is essentially reflective, non-judgemental and developmental. This problem has not just been confined to the policies of school leaders. Several teachers, especially in the initial stages of coaching, have said things such as:

> I can't really be bothered with all this tactful questioning and skirting around the issue. If I have done something wrong, then just tell me... and I want to know if my lesson was a Grade 1, 2, 3 or 4.

One of the fundamental successes of the project is that this challenge has been tackled so effectively that in most of the schools there has been a significant improvement in the perceived status of coaching. The crucial factor in this success has been the structure of the development programme for coaches. The programme has stressed the importance of self-reflection, showing that if teachers rely on other observers to point out their strengths and weaknesses, they will never be able to improve their own practice when they are not being observed or coached. One teacher, who was initially cynical about the whole coaching process, wrote after a session of coaching conversations:

> It was good to be able to discuss my lesson in a non-judgemental way with a colleague who was not my line manager. I learned much more this way than I have done from conventional feedback.

Another factor that helped to raise the credibility of coaching was the use of multiple coaching sessions. This involved groups of teachers conducting coaching conversations simultaneously in the same room with the LA consultant present to advise, reassure and provide guidance. In this way, the consultant was able to monitor the quality of the coaching and give instant feedback on its effectiveness. After one of these multiple coaching sessions, a teacher wrote about the 'really positive working atmosphere. Everywhere in the room there were colleagues deeply engaged in quality conversations about learning.'

The regular involvement of LA consultants in the coaching process at classroom level also helped to raise the profile of coaching and to keep the momentum going, so that coaching became an integral part of everyday practice and not just something that was done occasionally on professional development days or in after-school twilight sessions. Due to the goodwill generated by coaching events in attractive venues and respect for the 'hands-on' approach of the LA consultants, there were hardly any problems with teachers' willingness to invite observers into their classrooms as coaches.

The result of these developments is that, over the five school terms of the project's lifespan, the importance of coaching increased in the eyes of secondary teachers, particularly senior leaders. In most schools there was more recognition that coaching was an effective alternative to a hierarchical, judgemental model. One school dedicated one of the three annual lesson observations to a coaching model, where no judgements were made and instead a coaching conversation was conducted, which allowed both the observer and observed to reflect openly on teaching and learning issues. Three other schools decided to coach all their staff (two have already done so and one has arranged to do so), so that the skills involved in this kind of dialogue can be used as a regular mechanism in whole-school improvement.

Impact of the project

To assess the impact of the project, it is helpful to return to the distinction made earlier in the baseline evaluation between products, processes and outcomes. In all three of these areas, it was clear that good progress had been made by the end of the project.

Products were:

- All 'schools causing concern' in the LA (six involved in the project and one other identified as such at a later stage) included the development of a coaching programme as an action point in their plans, which were reviewed at the half-termly meetings which involved senior leaders from the school, governors and senior members of the LA's school improvement team. Before the project, none of these schools had this as an action point.
- A *Guide to Whole School Development* booklet was produced by the LA's secondary team and was shared with all the LA's schools (and also with some other local authorities). This booklet guides schools through the process of setting up sustainable coaching programmes.
- Teachers involved in the coaching programmes were provided with a template for recording impact and given guidance in how to complete it, with teachers from all the schools involved producing case studies showing clearly the impact of coaching on their practice as teachers and on the achievements of pupils.

Processes were:

- In total, 160 teachers have learned the principles of coaching and have had opportunities to practise their coaching skills. Before the project commenced there were fewer than 20 teachers across the LA who had been developed as coaches. These 160 teachers came from the six 'schools causing concern' targeted in both phases of the project, plus a further five secondary schools who had some involvement in phase 2. This meant that 11 of the LA's 15 mainstream secondary schools were involved in the *Effective Practices in CPD* project.
- Seven secondary schools had a regular cross-curricular coaching group. Members learned and applied the principles of coaching and conducted regular lesson reviews and coaching conversations. Four other secondary schools had particular subject departments or working groups involved in a regular coaching programme.
- The importance of coaching in secondary schools was shown by the greater integration of coaching into the regular processes of the school. As mentioned earlier, several schools now regard coaching as an effective alternative to hierarchical, judgemental lesson observations. Three of the seven 'schools causing concern' were developing all of their teachers in coaching and expecting them to include this as one of their CPD targets. Another school had replaced one of its regular rounds of 'judgemental' observations with a coaching conversation.

As one assistant head, whose response was typical among senior leaders, acknowledged at the end of the project:

I must admit I was sceptical about coaching at the start, but this project has shown me it really can make a difference to how teachers perform in the classroom.

Outcomes (impact) were:

- Before the project, there was no formal way for evaluating the impact of coaching. Evidence of impact was limited to vague statements from teachers that they had learned a lot from the coaching and that they had enjoyed the coaching conversations. Teachers now regularly produce evaluations of the impact of coaching on their work and the quality of these is improving all the time. They were also producing these more independently, with less guidance from the LA consultant. Teachers from all of the seven main project schools have produced evidence of impact in this way. This is partly the result of an evolving and improving method for assessing the impact, with the impact evaluation sheets devised in the LA being changed so that they now show clearly the 'before' and 'after' positions, for both the teachers' practice and the pupils' learning. This process has helped to establish a clear link between the CPD activity and specific improvement in learning at classroom level. So, in this way, coaching can be seen to work.
- For those teachers using coaching as a means to develop their practice in AfL, the National Strategy AfL review grids were another way to evaluate their progress. Many of the teachers involved in this way have improved their practice against the measures indicated in the AfL lesson review grids, now showing aspects of 'establishing' or 'enhancing' where they had previously been 'developing'. One particular aspect of this improved AfL practice has been the increased quality of pupils' contributions to the discussion about and setting of success criteria. Several schools had this as an AfL target and their lesson observation review grids show this has been an increasingly strong feature of those involved in the coaching programmes. The example of a grid in Table 6.1, plus the explanation which follows, help to illustrate this point.

Table 6.1: Reviewing learning and teaching in lessons (AfL focus)

Traffic light the statements:
Green = secure or surpassed
Amber = partial or inconsistent
Red = not evident

Teacher: NS	Subject: **English**	Class: **7**	Date: **29/4/08**
	Focusing	**Developing**	**Establishing**	**Enhancing**

	Focusing	**Developing**	**Establishing**	**Enhancing**
Pupils	All pupils know there are learning objectives. Most know what they have to do, a few have a limited understanding of what they are trying to learn. Some pupils can relate the lesson to recent lessons. Most pupils can work together. Some are confident about contributing to discussions. Some are confident about talking about their work. Most pupils make progress in their learning.	Most pupils are clear about what they are trying to learn. Many are aware of some features of a good learning outcome. Many can, with support, identify some strengths and weaknesses in their work and suggest how to improve it. Many recognise how their learning builds upon earlier learning. In whole-class discussions all pupils listen to others. Many are confidently able to contribute. In paired or group discussions most pupils contribute and learn from each other. Discussions remain focused. Most pupils make progress in relation to the learning objectives.	*All pupils have a clear understanding of what they are trying to learn (and value having learning objectives). All pupils are clear about the success criteria and can, with support, use these to judge the quality of their own and each others' work and identify how best to improve it. Most pupils can, with support, contribute to determining the success criteria.* All pupils can relate their learning to past, present and future learning in the subject and most can relate this learning to other subjects. In whole-class, group or paired discussions all pupils develop their thinking and learn from each other. Pupils are confidently able to take risks by sharing partially formed thinking or constructively challenging others. All pupils make good progress, in relation to the learning objectives, with some independence.	All pupils understand what they are trying to learn and confidently discuss this using subject terminology. All pupils routinely determine and use their own success criteria to improve. Pupils understand how their learning relates to the key concepts and skills they are developing. Pupils value talk for learning and consciously use it to advance their thinking. There is a classroom buzz: pupils initiate and lead whole-class discussions; group discussions are self-determined and governed. Responses are typically extended, demonstrate high-level thinking and support their views. All pupils have an appetite for learning: they independently identify and take their next steps in learning to make good progress.

Table 6.1 is an extract from an AfL review grid used in a secondary school. It was used as a guide during the coaching conversation between a teacher and her coach which followed a lesson observation. Both coach and coachee agreed that specific features were evident in the lesson (they shaded the grid in green, amber or red) and that the two features in italics in the 'Establishing' column were areas for development. Three months later, a subsequent observation with the same class and a follow-up coaching conversation showed that progress had been made in these areas. Pupils were discussing the success criteria for instructional writing and using these criteria to do peer- and self-assessment at regular points in the lesson. So this time the features that were italicised on the grid in the first observation were now improved. This was one of many examples where the AfL review grids helped to measure progress brought about by coaching.

Coaching was now having an impact on several aspects of teaching and learning. As well as improved practice in AfL, which had been a focus in both phases of the project, there have been at least two schools where measurable impact in written Literacy and in Speaking and Listening has been shown to be a direct result of coaching.

An effective use of baseline information in the evaluations of impact was something that only really emerged in the second phase of the programme. It is true to say that the work in the first phase did have some positive features. The evaluation process clearly showed the impact of coaching at classroom level and in this respect was partially successful. Teachers, using the first evaluation sheet produced, were able to demonstrate that the coaching programme had not only enhanced their own pedagogical practice but had also enabled specific groups of pupils to improve their learning. Teachers were able to identify concrete examples of impact. An example of an evaluation sheet completed at the end of the first phase is given in Table 6.2.

However, these phase 1 evaluations were not clear about the extent of the impact because they did not state plainly enough what the (baseline) position had been prior to the coaching. It is not clear in Example 1 what these Year 7 pupils were able (or not able) to do before the teacher was involved in the coaching. It was thus impossible to assess the true difference made by this particular CPD activity. Therefore, teachers involved in phase 2 started to use a different impact evaluation sheet, on which the progress made by individual teachers and by groups of pupils were highlighted more effectively by using a 'Before' and 'After' approach.

The second example (see Table 6.3) was taken at the end of the project.

Table 6.2: Example 1: Measuring progression in coaching – individual coach

Coach: JM   Coachee: DS

	Knowledge/ understanding of coach	Practice of coach	Impact on practice of coachee	Impact on pupils of coachee
Degree of impact	*Coach has been trained in principles of coaching.*	*Coach has coached at least one other teacher.*	*Coachee has implemented an idea from the coaching conversation.*	*Evidence produced to show that the idea from the coaching conversation has had an impact on pupil standards.*
Evidence/ example	Training session with LA consultant in December 2007.	Observed and coached by JM in January/ February 2008.	Discussion with JM in coaching conversation. Saw JM had used very precise success criteria in his lesson and used/ adapted his model.	Year 7 use the success criteria when completing written assessments to give a more comprehensive written response.

Table 6.3: Example 2: The impact of coaching

Name of coachee: Jack   Coached by: Sarah

Idea developed in coaching conversation

Use of literacy as an important feature of the lesson – VCOP* approach

	Before coaching	After coaching
Impact on practice of teacher	Would usually just focus on subject skills, with literacy being incidental.	Literacy now more explicit. Does starters which are devoted entirely to developing literacy, through the subject context, helping to highlight the importance of the literacy elements.
Impact on performance of pupils	Pupils were writing in paragraphs which linked sentences on the same topics, but with little overall structure or use of signposting.	Focus on openings and connectives has helped pupils to produce more rounded paragraphs.

* VCOP is a guide for helping pupils to make progress with vocabulary, connectives, openings and punctuation.

In this second example there is a useful distinction made between impact upon the practice of the teacher and impact upon the performance of pupils. Additionally, though, this time there is a baseline description for both, so the progress made by pupils was clearer and more measurable.

Overall judgement on the project's success

Although the project was successful overall, there were two main areas in which the first phase of the project could have been more successful, namely an increased focus on emotional literacy in the coaching programme and more effective use of baseline information to make the evaluation of impact sharper. Both of these areas were taken into account and improved in the project's second phase.

In some cases the impact of the project exceeded expectations. This was found in the extent to which some schools came to regard coaching as a regular alternative to the hierarchical observation model and also in the quality of the self-evaluations of impact which teachers were producing by the end of the programme. Teachers and senior leaders were increasingly realising that coaching was an excellent method of CPD because it is sustainable, self-reflective and impacts directly upon classroom practice. The ability of the *Effective Practices in CPD* project to demonstrate and show evidence of these successes was a crucial factor in this respect.

So there were definite learning points during the duration of the two phases of the project. The project will now be used to further develop effective CPD in the area. In the future the intention is to use the large number of positive cases from the project as a means of persuading senior leaders and teachers of the value of coaching. This will help to extend the programme into new schools and to sustain and widen the programme in existing schools.

Features of effective professional development

In considering the features of effective professional development, the following were definitely in place:

- The need for clarity of purpose at the outset in CPD activity
All participating schools were clear that the coaching programme should result in improved pupil outcomes, not just changed practices by teachers.

- The value of a specific focus and goal for CPD activity, aligned to clear timescales

The inclusion of the development of coaching in the action plans of key schools gave the programme a clear focus and timescales that were monitored regularly by school leaders.

- The importance of CPD activity including a focus on pupil outcomes

Being able to demonstrate improved pupil outcomes helped to convince key people of the value of coaching.

- The need to develop participants' ownership of CPD activity

The value placed on teachers' self-reflection in coaching gave them a strong sense of ownership of the programme.

- The value of time for reflection and feedback

The whole programme was built around the principle of securing time for detailed reflection on teaching and learning.

- The significance of collaborative CPD

The coaching pairs and trios ensured that collaboration was at the heart of the process.

- The importance of strategic leadership of CPD

Gaining the active support of senior leaders in schools was vital for ensuring the momentum of the coaching programmes.

- Understanding how to evaluate the impact of CPD

The increased use of baseline measures enabled the evaluations of impact to become more precise and robust as the project developed.

All these developments have led to a widespread acceptance in the LA that not only is coaching an integral CPD activity, but also of the idea that there should be a regular mechanism for evaluating its impact. Overall, the project has left a lasting legacy of skill, understanding and goodwill within secondary schools and the local authority, on which extensive future progress in teaching and learning can be built.

Chapter 7

Coaching in a special school: making teachers and support staff feel more valued

Sara Bubb

Context

This special school is very successful: it was deemed outstanding by Ofsted in 2007. It has a stable staff of about 50 people, including 12 teachers and 22 teaching assistants. Working at the school are three very experienced assistant heads (no deputy), one trainee on the Graduate Teacher Programme (GTP), and two newly qualified teachers (NQTs); the remaining teachers are middle leaders. This school has had strong professional development provision for the last five years during which time there has been a particular commitment to counselling, mentoring and coaching. For instance, the Ofsted report (2007) says that, 'Teaching assistants make a valuable contribution to the quality of teaching. Several have undertaken advanced training to support learning and all undergo regular professional development. Some teaching assistants have additional skills such as counselling which are used to good effect.'

Phase 1 project

Since 2002 the senior leadership team (SLT) had been interested in emotional literacy for students and staff. The school was involved in another TDA-funded project on mentoring before the *Effective Practices in CPD* project, so the coaching-mentoring ethos was well embedded. In this project, an organisation developed the staff in coaching using the GROW model. This fitted in with the school's approach to helping students manage their behaviour because it was about them making choices about pursuing different courses of action. The coaching was not related to performance management.

Aims

The project's main aim was for all staff who wanted it to be coached by a coach from outside the school and to link this, where appropriate, to progress in meeting the National Professional and Occupational Standards.

The project funding was spent on employing an external coach who came to the school for a day once a fortnight. The 50-minute sessions were available for any staff and happened during school time.

Impact of phase 1

The first phase of the project was deemed to be very successful by the project leader, who wrote:

> *We have seen significant development of a number of staff and are now at a stage where we can develop an innovative middle management structure where people with teaching and learning responsibility payments lead teams of staff with the focus of supporting, developing and resourcing learning rather than being subject or faculty focused.*

A total of 19 staff (39 per cent) were coached, of whom:

- 10 were teachers (out of a total of 12)
- three were administrative staff
- six were support staff.

Ten were new to the experience.

The classification of CPD into processes and outcomes (there were no outputs or products) was used to identify the project's *baseline* position and the overall outcomes or *impact* made.

Processes

Development needs, including coaching and mentoring, were identified in appraisal (support staff) and performance management (teachers). For teachers, the objectives set were related to the Professional Standards and were reflected in the CPD plan and were the focus of the coaching. The impact of coaching and mentoring was discussed in the autumn review meetings.

Interestingly, most staff began with coaching, and then moved to mentoring or a blend of coaching and mentoring once they identified their needs in the coaching sessions.

Outcomes (impact) for staff

The coach judged that from the baseline position there were 'positive tangible outcomes' for 16 of the 19 members of staff who were coached and that 'This demonstrates that the coaching model and investment in staff development has been effective'. The project leader considered that there were significant outcomes from coaching and mentoring for individuals such as:

- A TA attended a briefing about higher level teaching assistant (HLTA) status and intended to start this next year.
- Two teachers moved up to take on teaching and learning responsibilities (TLR) (see Example 1 below).
- One TA started a Graduate Teacher Programme (GTP).
- One teacher is looking for their next post.
- A teacher has left the school, having decided that teaching was not for him.
- The site manager became much clearer about how to manage his assistant.
- Administrative staff are clearer about their roles and the admin team functions more efficiently.
- The project leader had four coaching sessions as a result of which he decided not to go for headships but to stay put and do a higher degree. He is studying staff development impact for his doctoral dissertation.

However, it is hard to attribute these outcomes to the coaching alone and little hard evidence was offered.

Example 1: Impact on teacher

One teacher had two coaching sessions and follow-up emails. She was an experienced teacher, but as the wife of a man in the Services she had moved around from school to school, country to country but never looking for promotion. The coaching helped her to consider this: 'It made me focus on getting a career for the first time.' As a result she applied for and got a teaching and learning responsibility (TLR) within the school.

Outcomes (impact) for pupils

The project leader cited two tangible effects on pupils as a result of staff coaching:

- a redeveloped tuck shop and healthy schools initiative
- better RE provision in the school as a result of the RE teacher starting the GTP.

However, as the coaching occurred within the school day the question of disruption to the learning of these pupils must be explored, especially as they have emotional and learning needs.

The school evaluated the project using what they call a 'causation trail' that starts with performance management or appraisal and ends with the review of impact (see Table 7.1).

Table 7.1: Causation trail – an example

Causation trail period 2007–2008

We are reviewing the coaching and mentoring we have provided as part of staff professional learning and development. Could you fill out this questionnaire if you are happy to comment on any coaching or mentoring that relates to work-based practice.

Link from performance management
To develop responsibility for managing the tuck shop as part of the healthy schools initiative
Link to professional standards
Health and well-being
C22   Know the current legal requirements, national policies and guidance on the safeguarding and promotion of the well-being of children and young people.
Teamworking and collaboration
C40 Work as a team member and identify opportunities for working with colleagues, managing their work where appropriate and sharing the development of effective practice with them.

Please describe the aspect of your work practice you focused on.
Getting healthy tuck shop started; produce, prices, adhering to government guidelines. Managing TA in charge of tuck shop.

How did the coaching change your thinking in this area?
Became more logical and methodical when planning new venture.

How did your practice change?
My thinking became more focused, and meetings with TA in charge of tuck shop were purposeful.

Can you identify ways this has impacted upon pupils?
Directly: *Healthier diet at break times, making choices, some have taken responsibility for running the tuck shop.*
Indirectly: *Exposure to new and varied healthy alternatives to crisps as a snack, life skills such as handling money, keeping to sell by dates, etc.*

Link to performance review and anticipated performance management outcomes
Tuck shop has been a success and is breaking even, pupils are enjoying the variety of food on offer and many have tried new things. TA in charge of tuck shop is enjoying running it and feels it has been a great success.
Use of KS4 pupils to help run tuck shop needs to be looked at and needs to become more structured.
Rubbish from snacks needs to be kept to a minimum.

Phase 2 project

The project continued from the first phase so the baseline was as described above.

Aims

This phase of the project aimed to ensure that coaching was sustainable for the future – by developing expert coaches and middle leaders and continuing to develop how to demonstrate the outcomes of coaching.

Some parts of the phase 2 project plan happened and others didn't. The following was planned and did happen.

Table 7.2

Activities	Timeline	Cost
Two-day coaching course was run in-house on school days by an external facilitator. Eleven staff took part and coached each other: six teachers: two SLT, four middle leaders five support staff: special educational needs coordinators (SENCO), two music therapists, one play therapist, bursar.	Autumn 2008 One development day (two weeks to coach each other). Half-day training (two weeks to coach each other). Half-day training.	Fee to trainer + cover
Five days' training over a year for a high-level coaching qualification (ILM5) for three of the leadership team (headteacher and two assistant headteachers). The training is run at the school with just one other attendee.	Spring 2009 to Autumn 2009. Two training days have taken place.	Fee + cover

The following was planned but did not happen.

Table 7.3

Supply cover to enable assistant headteachers to coach middle leaders Four one-hour sessions for each of the four middle leaders = 16 hours + half day to evaluate coaching Supply at six hours per day = total hours 21 or three-and-a-half days	Autumn 2008 – Spring 2009
Performance management training for middle management TLR holders	Spring 2009

In summary, the following activities occurred:

- Eleven staff have had a two-day introductory coaching course.
- Three senior staff have started the Institute of Leadership and Management level 5 coaching course.
- The joint development day with the federation of local schools included a one-and-a-half day session on coaching.
- Governors have had an introductory two-hour coaching session.

The intention was to embed these activities by using expert coaches to coach from summer 2009.

Impact of phase 2

By the end of the funding, the project leader felt that although the project had been successful, it could not be considered very successful because the middle management training had not taken place. Performance management training had been set up for the summer term 2009.

The focus of the extension to the project was to make coaching sustainable by not relying on external coaching but to develop expert coaching at the school. The project leader said:

> We have a well-developed understanding amongst staff of the benefits of coaching. We have consolidated the role of coaching in the school and are now in a strategic position in terms of governors and leadership to move coaching forward. Eight staff are now coaching others.

The SLT have spotted emotional intelligence in individuals that they hadn't appreciated before. The headteacher considers that teachers and support staff feel more valued because of the investment in them. She believes:

> There has been a cultural shift in the way that students are spoken to and about. Staff give them time to calm down. Coaching has helped them work with youngsters.

There have also been unintended benefits. The project leader said:

> An indirect impact has been that several other special schools have sought our advice on developing coaching and the local authority is using us as a coaching centre of expertise.

Outcomes (impact) for staff

- Middle and senior staff indicated that they had a much more developed understanding of coaching and its impact upon staff and pupils (see Examples 2 and 3).
- Staff had a developing understanding of how they could use coaching with students during lessons and to support their social and emotional development (see Examples 2 and 3).

Outcomes (impact) for pupils

The headteacher's observations indicated that staff had developed their use of questioning with the pupils and that pupils were able to offer more sophisticated responses to questions during the plenary. She said:

> Staff now do more listening and questioning rather than telling – empowering the students to get the answers themselves.

Pupils now mentored each other. Eight Year 11 students were asked or volunteered to mentor and had received some training in looking after younger pupils. They were going to help train Year 10 mentors. They supervised 'quiet lunch' with a teacher and were used at flash points: they ran after pupils who tried to run off to stop them escaping. One mentor said:

> It's good to talk to them about their interests to calm them down, then they talk about their problems.

This had an impact upon the younger pupils: there were fewer fights. The impact on the Year 11 students was significant, especially in terms of self-esteem. They wore their badges with pride. They said:

> Watching adults and being mentors has helped us be mentors and behave better.

> We don't react as quick when people use bad language.

> Hearing others swear makes me realise the effect of my bad language on others.

They questioned and listened so that pupils came to answers themselves.

The project leader admitted, 'Proving outcomes is hard.' He used a spreadsheet to record who was being coached or mentored (distinguishing between the two) each term and to record individual outcomes. However, he only recorded that there were coaching sessions in a term but not the number of sessions. The school improvement partner was also asked to monitor the impact of coaching.

Overall judgement on the project's success

The project had clearly been a success in that staff were using coaching techniques with each other and with pupils. The project leader identified three issues that had been successfully addressed in the second phase of the project:

1. 'Staff were seeing the coaching sessions as an opportunity to get counselling for personal problems in phase 1 so we needed to get it more professional.' The coach had overstepped personal boundaries.
2. Coaching needed to become sustainable. This was not the case when an external expert was doing the coaching.
3. The senior staff faced an ethical issue about who should coach whom and whether the roles should be kept separate from performance management (PM). It was decided to keep the coaching role and that of the PM reviewer separate and that different people would carry out these roles.

The project leader considered that having bespoke development by experts on site was highly cost effective. However, this is debatable because all the CPD sessions and coaching happened within the school day, not on development days, after school or at other times, thus disrupting pupils and costing a great deal in cover. On-site CPD sessions also meant that there was no opportunity for staff to network with people from outside the school.

Regarding next steps the project leader said:

> Whilst continuing the training of staff as expert coaches we now need to embed and consolidate new practices. We want to run the system for a year with coaching needs identified in PM, then have coaching/observations/causation trails and then back to PM. We want to get to the stage where staff ask for coaching. We are looking at how we can offer coaching advice and support to other schools through our outreach provision.

Example 2: two support staff

Impact upon them: The two music therapists were sceptical about the coaching training at first. One said, 'Why were we taking time out from the kids? But I learned loads and it was very beneficial.' They appreciated the time to understand processes better and became clearer about the differences between mentoring, coaching and therapy. One was given a book to help him address the confusion between them – what he called 'toilet reading' in that it was done in contemplative moments. The penny dropped! They appreciated the structured time to practise coaching: one did so with the bursar and both got a lot out of it.

Impact on pupils: The music therapists say that coaching techniques – questioning, listening, being comfortable with silence – are becoming part of their unconscious repertoire.

> When a kid's kicking off we just go for a walk and using coaching methods e.g. 'We're going to walk around the field until you're ready… Do you want to talk about it?… What are your options?… Where do you want to go from here?'

They use coaching in their teaching of music technology too.

As a result of their increased belief and confidence in coaching, they are now running a counselling group of six Year 7 to 10 boys for an hour a week, and use the GROW model to help the students identify where they are and where they want to get to. One of the support staff said, 'To begin with they didn't know what to expect but even at the end of the first session kids were hugging each other – it was amazing.'

Example 3: Teacher

Impact on her: This teacher already had 30 credits from a counselling course but felt that the training in coaching was very beneficial:

> The training was excellent, it moved me on further. I realised that I wasn't doing coaching and mentoring as well as I thought I was. I have to go into coaching mode, because it's not quite second nature yet. It's more instinctive for me to do with pupils than with adults. I do do it with the NQT but it's harder with more experienced teachers. With the NQT I now say things like 'How do you think your folder is going?' instead of telling her what to do and giving her a list of jobs.

Impact on pupils: She has used a coaching style with a girl with emotional and behavioural problems who squeezes her hard when hugging her. Instead of telling her to stop, the teacher says:

> *'How do think I feel when you squeeze me so tight?'*

> *'You hate me.'*

> *'Is that what you think?'*

> *'Maybe not.'*

This has helped the pupil behave more appropriately.

Impact on her personal life: The coaching has had benefits for her personal life:

> *I've used it with my husband – he really appreciates it (but doesn't realise I'm doing it!). It's helped him prioritise.*

She has also used a coaching style with her teenage daughter:

> *I ask her reflective type questions to help her edit her homework. So it works with mainstream children.*

Features of effective professional development

In considering features of effective professional development, these were in place:

- The value of time for reflection and feedback

Coaching had been heavily invested in and those staff involved had a great deal of time for reflection. As one member of staff said, 'the most precious commodity is time.'

- The significance of collaborative CPD

However, about one-half of the staff were not involved in any of the phases of the coaching projects at all.

- The importance of strategic leadership of CPD

Coaching had been strategically led, planned and managed to a degree, but there had been no targeting of people or teams where coaching would have been most useful.

- Participants' ownership of CPD activity

The optional nature of the coaching activities had resulted in ownership by those involved, but many staff were not and so perhaps coaching had been divisive.

However, these features were not sufficiently in place or required more thought:

- The need for clarity of purpose at the outset in CPD activity

It was not entirely clear why coaching was so important, why they needed to do more of it or how its impact would be measured. Coaching for a purpose related to pupils and a focus on intended impact was needed.

- The value of a specific focus and goal for CPD activity, aligned to clear timescales

The time frames went beyond the end of the project deadline and there was no clear goal for coaching. It was seen more as an end in itself rather than to improve anything specific.

- Understanding how to evaluate the impact of CPD

There were no specific success criteria or clear vision of exactly what needed to be better and why or how much coaching across the year was to be expected. The coaching was entirely optional so nobody was targeted for this development activity. It may be that the staff who were coached were not the ones who needed it most. For instance, two support staff were music therapists so presumably already had skills in this area, and one of the teachers had already been on an accredited counselling course.

There was monitoring of who had been coached and mentored but not of who was acting as a coach. There was no accountability framework and little monitoring of the external coach. Trust was not enough because the coaching strayed too far beyond the professional into the personal.

- The importance of CPD activity including a focus on pupil/student outcomes

Any impact on pupils was a by-product rather than a focus.

- The importance of engaging with a variety of CPD opportunities

The project only looked at coaching.

- More staff needed to be involved and people targeted strategically.
- Time: all the coaching has happened within the school day, not after school or on development days, and thus the effect on pupils' education and well-being would be worth evaluating.

Chapter 8

Motivating with Maths

Margaret Mulholland

Context

This project was based in a one-form entry, inner city primary school serving an area of high social disadvantage. The percentage of pupils from minority ethnic backgrounds is well above average, with the largest group being pupils of Black African origin. A high percentage of pupils speak English as an additional language. Punjabi is the most common first language among these pupils. The proportion of pupils with learning difficulties is above average.

Phase 1 project

The focus of the curriculum had been on the development of literacy skills. Now the school felt they needed to raise the profile of Maths, developing the knowledge, skills and understanding of all staff and thus raise standards. The Ofsted inspection in January 2007 confirmed the school's concerns that attainment levels in Maths needed to rise. The project leader was very clear from the outset about the need for 'long-term and sustainable impact on teachers' skills and understanding'. The school identified key questions to address through the project.

- Can high-quality and sustainable CPD contribute to raising standards in Maths?
- What impact will modelling lessons, team teaching and peer observations have on the quality of teaching and learning in Maths?
- Will diagnosing children's errors and misconceptions contribute to raising standards?
- What impact will collaborative learning have on children's levels of motivation and engagement in Maths activities?
- Can the thinking and problem-solving skills developed in Maths be transferred to other areas of the curriculum?

- How can we successfully record and disseminate the impact of this project to other schools?

Aim

The aim of the first phase of the project was to enrich the professional development of colleagues in the teaching of Maths and support the mathematical thinking and reasoning of pupils. The project's objectives were to:

- Raise standards in Maths through developing a problem-solving approach in lessons.
- Work with staff to develop their understanding of children's misconceptions and their ability to diagnose errors.
- Research the use of models and images to consolidate children's understanding of key mathematical concepts.
- Promote collaborative learning, creative problem-solving and speaking and listening skills.

Success criteria were discussed at the outset of the project and were listed as follows:

- The quality of the teaching and learning in Maths throughout the school will have improved (although it was not specified in what ways or by how much).
- The whole staff will have benefited from the input of consultants and will have enhanced their practice in the classroom through joint planning, team teaching, peer observations and the application of innovative styles of teaching and assessment for learning techniques.
- Staff will have had the opportunity to reflect on the areas they need to develop as the project progresses.
- Staff will be directly involved in setting their own targets.
- The standards achieved by children across the school will have risen to ensure we exceed the challenging targets set by our local authority *and* maintain predicted levels of progress for all our children.

Some staff members felt that they needed support in planning, teaching and assessing learning in Maths. They wanted a sustained package of CPD activity that would have a real impact upon their practice, rather than a one-off course.

Staff members had attended a variety of different courses, but they didn't always have the opportunity to share what they learnt. Teachers in the early years of their career were not always given the opportunity to work alongside or learn from more experienced teachers. The school had had a stable staff for many years, but an influx of less experienced teachers into this small school had had a notable impact.

You realise that you need to keep revisiting good practice as new staff haven't 'been there yet' and long-term staff have become complacent.
(Head)

The project worked in partnership with 'Be a Mathematician' (BEAM), a mathematical publisher and consultancy dedicated to the development of thinking skills in Maths. CPD opportunities for the whole school community led by BEAM consultants were the focus over the life cycle of the project. The school used project funding to buy in blocks of time with consultants. Consultant-led workshops focused on strategies to improve the teaching and learning of Maths: modelling, problem-solving, use of games, competitions and designing resources.

Teaching assistants were involved in CPD sessions, and parental involvement was encouraged. Parents were invited to Maths workshops to learn about the strategies that were being introduced to the classroom. Processes used during the workshops included modelling by the consultant in the classroom and team observations; e.g. Foundation Stage staff, including the TAs and learning support assistant, would work with the BEAM consultant in the morning and then the KS2 team would work with him in the afternoon. In between consultant visits the staff would practise their new strategies using peer observation and team teaching, and a portion of meeting time would be given to progress reviews for teachers using new strategies and approaches.

As the staff's confidence developed, teachers worked with the consultant to identify and prioritise specific strategies for their classes, developing teaching materials and tools. The school received a detailed calculations policy from the Borough, and, by the end of phase 1 they had the confidence to adapt the policy to reflect the good practice being developed at the school.

Impact of phase 1

The outcomes for teachers included improvements in planning and pedagogy, making Maths relevant and accessible, making speaking and listening targets explicit, identifying pupils' baseline in order to support progress and an emphasis on mathematical language. Support staff were particularly aware of the need to avoid giving answers, and to ask questions to lead children to the solutions for themselves. They now understood the importance of allowing the children to explain how they work things out and to use this information to help with questioning them and moving their learning on.

Never give an answer, always ask a question. This is our new mantra.

(TA)

All members of staff were now aware of the importance of using – and encouraging the children to use – the correct Maths vocabulary in all lessons. The outcomes for teachers also included improvements in their teaching and pedagogy, the use of modelling and pattern, critical thinking with children, and identifying and removing barriers to learning.

These child-centred ways of working put the focus back on the importance of ongoing assessment for learning. It also reminded teachers of the need to plan for the time they spent with groups of children or individuals and to work out their level of understanding before deciding on the steps to move them on.

Pupil outcomes included a greater self-awareness in learning and improved confidence. There was evidence of children being far more confident in using a range of speaking and listening strategies to justify their ideas, and there was an obvious sense of fun and enjoyment in participating in Maths 'debates', as evidenced in classroom observations and from comments made by the children themselves.

In short, the first year of the project inspired staff and resulted in far more collaborative learning and problem-solving approaches being used in classes: however, there was still a lot of work to be done to become a 'conjecturing community'.

Questionnaires filled in by all teaching and support staff showed that the project had been very thought provoking and had challenged the way in which teachers planned their lessons and their interactions with pupils, further evidenced by the improvement in pupil attainment across Key Stages (see later).

I saw some children, not necessarily the most able, bloom with confidence when class discussions focused more on how you could approach a problem, rather than supply an answer.

(Year 3 teacher)

Staff feedback was used to plan the second phase of the project work with consultants, colleagues and parents.

Phase 2 project

BEAM training in phase 1 raised awareness of the different techniques and strategies that can be used to enhance the quality of Maths teaching and learning. Although regular review and evaluation meetings had been held as part of phase 1, members of staff felt that time needed to be built into the project to allow all members of the class team, including teachers, TAs and learning mentors to review the learning together and to give feedback to each other on the strengths of a particular lesson and the progress made by the children.

The school used the project funding to release staff for further CPD activity. Since the project began, outside consultants held 24 CPD sessions with school staff, e.g. two-day cycles of workshops for staff and TAs. These took the form of twilight sessions and day workshops, with consultants working with teachers in the classroom.

> We would have two supply teachers in for the day and they would cover staff in rotation as they worked with the consultant.
>
> (Project leader)

Consultants led further twilight sessions involving TAs.

> It has made such a difference to us and the way we work, we understand now what the teacher is working towards and why. I think we can do so much more to help the children understand, rather than tell them the answer so they could keep up with the rest of the class.
>
> We are being encouraged to observe lessons with the older children so that we know what comes next and why they need to be able to recognise numbers before leaving the nursery.
>
> (TA in nursery)

External visits were planned, e.g. a working party visiting other schools to share best practice.

The first phase of the project had relied almost exclusively on one 'superconsultant'. Phase 2 added new consultants with a wider range of approaches, for example, in classroom language, which applied to the curriculum beyond Maths. According to the headteacher, 'there has been informal development of mentoring', e.g. pairing experienced with less experienced staff during the CPD sessions.

Impact of phase 2

The outcomes for the project's second phase tended to refer to whole-school improvements, as there was little data available to *evaluate* the impact upon individual improvement in teaching, or on Key Stage attainment data. Teaching and learning in this school had improved overall as seen by more personalised learning and improvements in the questioning skills of teachers, TAs and learning mentors. These had been enhanced through the theory and practice explored by BEAM consultants with the whole school staff, e.g. De Bono's Thinking Hats and through revisiting Bloom's Taxonomy.

> *Over the term of the project I have become clearer about how I can use questioning to help the children see where they have gone wrong or where they have failed to understand a concept.*
>
> (Year 6 teacher)

There was also a wider repertoire of teaching skills and styles, raised expectations and consistency. There was a far greater expectation that children would be engaged in active speaking and listening in each session and regularly be required to repeat what a 'talk partner' has said. This expectation was now consistent throughout the school, from nursery to Year 6. Children were being challenged to reason and explain their work and to produce posters to communicate to others what they had been doing.

Greater pupil ownership was also an important outcome. Handing the explanations over to the children had been a very important piece of learning for the adults involved.

> *We have seen how powerful it is to give the children a sense of ownership over their Maths and to develop the expectation that all children will be required at some time to present their work.*
>
> (Year 4 teacher)

Project participants were making regular and far greater use of models and images, which proved to be very powerful learning tools for the children.

> *They are slowly beginning to understand the importance of how to learn as opposed to what to learn.*
>
> (Year 6 teacher)

There was also a shared language around learning:

> *The sessions, particularly the opportunity to view filmed team teaching sessions, have enabled us to realise the importance of not focusing on the children getting the answer right, but more on teaching the Maths and 'what is going on under the bonnet'.*
>
> (Project leader)

Teachers were much more aware of the importance of speaking and listening, and planned for whole sessions to be devoted to developing a particular skill, using a wide variety of new and exciting strategies or techniques to encourage 'talk'. Teachers and support staff had a bank of activities and suggestions for promoting talk such as 'Devil's advocate' and 'Ticket to explain'. There was also much greater use of open questions, such as: 'Why do you think you know that?' and 'How do you know?' This was evidenced in both the teachers' planning and in lesson observations. Teachers learnt that it was possible to differentiate an activity by making use of questioning.

The school was now closer to becoming 'a conjecturing community', where the adults did not step in too quickly to provide the right answer, but rather allowed the children to question, make suggestions and be guided towards working out problems for themselves. Problem-solving was now part of the big picture. On a recent visit a science inspector had noted how pupils were asking exploratory questions in science. This shows that the school had successfully adopted an enquiry-based approach to learning, not just seeing higher order questions as an extension task for more able students.

Consultant workshops had helped to raise parental confidence. Many parents claimed they could now better support their children's numeracy. Some parents agreed to work in the school on a weekly basis, playing Maths games with the children.

Wow, that was fantastic – Maths brought to life. Maths with humour and, amazingly, Maths made fun! This session not only gave me insight into how Maths is taught to my daughter in school, but taught me games to play with her at home to support her school work.

(Parent)

Overall judgement on the project's success

The project was successful. The school has clearly benefited from the focus on raising attainment in Maths. Results were broadly improving as evidenced by attainment data. Energy had been put into building and developing pedagogy, utilising external consultants. The project's focus on all adults working together to develop one area of the children's learning, rather than sending individuals on courses, meant that everyone was trialling similar ideas and techniques.

We are all speaking the same language and there is a raised awareness and a general 'buzz' around the subject of Mathematics.

(Project leader)

Developing one subject area at a time, in a sustained way, meant the school identified protected time for teachers and support staff for collaboration, application, reflection and review. Setting aside time to write in learning journals has enabled staff to internalise and assimilate what they have learnt and to reflect on its impact upon their practice and the children's learning. Taking the time to find out what children know and understand, and how they reached a particular conclusion, supported the delivery of personalised learning.

The project benefited from very high-quality opportunities for development, with excellent input from the external consultants and a focus on pupil outcomes through improved teaching and learning practices. CPD was implicit in this project. There would have been value in making the CPD processes (i.e. mentoring, collaborative learning) more explicit, so that they could be embedded into the school structure and staff behaviour. The project needed a strategy to embed the processes and products in a sustained model.

There is understandable risk with only utilising outside consultants for CPD – the learning can sometimes stay with those involved in the sessions, and there can be limited ownership of developing the outcomes within the school. Such a risk might feel more comfortable for a school with a history of established, stable staff (like this one), but becomes problematic if there is no strategy to embed effective approaches to CPD within a replicable and repeatable structure.

That said, the project had a direct and positive impact. There was a marked improvement in terms of children's achievement in Maths at all three Key Stages over the course of the project:

- 10 per cent increase in pupils achieving level 4 or above in the KS2 SATs
- 24 per cent increase in pupils achieving level 2 or above in KS1 SATs
- 23 per cent increase in pupils achieving six points or more in the aspect of Calculations in the Foundation Stage Profiles.

The project would have been even better if all colleagues in the school had defined what they wanted sustainable and high-quality CPD to look like in the context of their school, highlighting the need to identify CPD processes as they embarked on enhancing teaching and learning. The impact upon individuals and teams could have been mapped alongside the impact upon whole-school professional development. The school staff would have benefited from sharing greater responsibility for leading change (expertise was demonstrated by the project leader) rather than the energy and inspiration appearing to come almost exclusively from external experts.

However, according to the headteacher, 'We now have the confidence and the expertise to take this learning forward under our own steam.' The project helped the school identify that it had the internal expertise and capacity to lead CPD. External visits were planned and more work was required to embed processes and turn them into protocols.

The next steps for the project were summed up by the project leader:

Team planning, teaching and review sessions will continue, within the limitations of the school budget. Maths will continue to be a high priority within the school development plan, and as part of ongoing and sustained CPD.

Features of effective professional development

The processes by which teaching and learning can be improved without input from external consultants had been recognised (e.g. mentoring, team teaching, collaborative reflection, importance of development of the wider workforce, particularly TAs), but could have been developed. The school needed to be more strategic about methodology and evaluation – what strategies were in place for change and progress, and how they were to get there – so that CPD could then be built upon, refined, improved and embedded.

In considering the nine approaches and features of effective professional development, the following comments are offered across both project phases:

• The need for clarity of purpose at the outset in CPD activity

This was an important contributor to the project's success. The aims of the project provided a clear rationale behind which all staff could unite (Ofsted findings in 2007 helped to build the validity of these aims). Staff recognised the value of developing numeracy for whole-school improvement and individual professional development.

• The value of a specific focus and goal for CPD activity, aligned to clear timescales

CPD sessions led by external consultants were clearly defined and mapped across an 18-month time frame to ensure the development of whole-school knowledge and understanding about teaching and learning styles. Integration and incremental steps for TA and parental development were also defined.

• The importance of CPD activity including a focus on pupil outcomes

The emphasis on raising pupil attainment was the driving force and specific focus for this school. The type and style of CPD adopted by the school developed from the strategies identified *with* the consultants that staff believed would enhance pupil learning in Maths.

• The need to develop participants' ownership of CPD activity
This was less developed than anticipated, with some staff feeling they had relied too heavily on external consultants. However, the fact that all workshops had involved classroom modelling and/or collaborative teaching meant that teachers and TAs began to recognise the direct impact on their own practice and were very clear that the consultant's role was only that of an initiator. Staff questionnaires and interviews recognised the importance of taking responsibility for ongoing development. High expectations of staff communicated by the SLT helped to ensure progress and development work took place between the consultant visits.

• The importance of engaging with a variety of CPD opportunities
This was widening beyond the BEAM workshops, e.g. external visits, recognising internal skills, informal mentoring, modelling, collaborative teaching, planning and observation and good evidence of reflective practice using the reflective log.

• The value of time for reflection and feedback
This was achieved through the learning journal and post-lesson evaluations, which were seen as valuable. The most successful example of the value of reflection was perhaps the request by staff to have feedback and discussion from collaborative teaching sessions immediately after a lesson.

• The significance of collaborative CPD
This was developing as a recognised CPD process within the school. Use of collaborative teaching was limited to numeracy rather than as an acknowledged CPD strategy across the curriculum.

• The importance of strategic leadership of CPD
Although the project leader did provide strategic leadership, the project, while well managed, was demanding and difficult for the project leader to balance alongside other senior leadership responsibilities.

• Understanding how to evaluate the impact of CPD
The hard and soft evidence collected attributed many of the improved pupil outcomes to the new methods introduced by consultants. Staff gave less thought to the impact of CPD processes (e.g. mentoring) from which they had so clearly benefited. The exception was the TAs who cited their involvement in workshops, lesson observations and collaborative work as making a substantial improvement to the classroom support they provided. Establishing a baseline for pupil achievement would have revealed the size of the impact achieved.

Chapter 9

Professional development for early career teachers and support staff: evaluating impact

Sara Bubb

Context

This project took place in an 11–18 secondary school with just over 1,000 pupils, a large percentage of whom are known to be eligible for free school meals and are from minority ethnic backgrounds. The school has specialist business and enterprise status and is a training school: indeed, a quarter of current teachers trained at the school. In 2007 it was deemed outstanding by Ofsted.

Staff development had been well led by the deputy for many years. This involved the school in several TDA-funded projects and Teachers TV programmes. Inspectors judged, 'Professional development is pivotal to the school. Performance management is well established and the sharing of good practice and honest evaluation are highly valued.'

The project (phase 1 and 2)

Although the school had a strong professional development culture, the CPD leader felt that evaluating the impact of CPD was a weak link and so this was the priority throughout the project's two phases. There were two development initiatives which were specifically implemented and monitored for impact:

A   Development for classroom-based support staff.
B   Professional development for early career teachers (ECTs).

Aim

The aim was to continue to develop more effective CPD evaluation in order to improve the quality of future CPD opportunities and thus raise job satisfaction and pupil achievement. A questionnaire was designed and given to support staff at the start of the project and again at the end (see Appendix). It was given again at the end of the 2008–9 year in order to quantify progress.

The project leader was very specific about *objectives*. Through the project, she wanted to:

- introduce more choice of CPD activity – a menu for personalised learning and co-coaching
- evaluate the impact of the CPD menu upon teaching and learning
- further develop methods of evaluating the impact of CPD upon teaching and learning
- invite local schools to sessions
- embed the standards linked to performance management objectives
- continue to involve support staff (teaching assistants and learning support assistants) in evaluating impact and increasing the impact of their work upon teaching and learning
- continue to involve students in evaluating impact
- work with early professional development (EPD) teachers as a specific group to further develop skills
- disseminate findings.

Success criteria were seen as having:

- a menu of CPD choices in place
- measures to evaluate impact, e.g. tools, classroom observation, questionnaire (see Appendix)
- support staff and students contributing to evaluation through formal classroom observations as well as informal feedback
- staff with linked performance management objectives, and their co-coaching and CPD choices linked to the new standards
- EPD teachers supported in their development as evidenced in their professional development plans
- been disseminated via case studies and local CPD leaders meetings.

A. The support staff project

There were four half-day offsite CPD sessions for the 40–50 classroom-based support staff – teaching assistants, learning mentors, heads of year and technicians. Never before had all the classroom-based support staff participated in a CPD session together. One said, 'Just being together was powerful.' The focus of their development was on the difference they could make to the pupils in the classroom. This involved raising their confidence when talking to teachers because they were rather reticent. The session was led as far as possible by support staff themselves, with help from the project manager, who is also the CPD leader and deputy. They valued 'learning from each other', as one teaching assistant said.

Here is a flavour of the sessions:

Session 1
1. Support staff questionnaire
2. What makes a good teacher/good lesson: collection of ideas from support staff sessions
3. Delivering difficult messages to a teacher
4. Personal action plan.

Session 2
1. Beginnings and endings of lessons – gathering information
2. Feedback form
3. Practical tips for supporting learning in the classroom
4. Support staff skills audit.

They worked on improving people's skills and confidence in giving feedback to teachers. In groups they discussed questions such as these (Table 9.1):

Table 9.1

How many of your group have observed a lesson and given feedback?
For those who have, was it written or verbal?
What kind of feedback was given?
Do you think the feedback was taken on board by the teacher? How do you know?
Any tips? What advice would you give to other support staff, here or at another school? What went well? Could anything have made it better?
If you have not given feedback what stopped you? What would need to be changed to enable you to do this?

They role-played giving tricky messages, starting off with working out how to comment sensitively about someone's hair looking a mess and then moved into the classroom setting to solve problems such as:

A student isn't working and the teacher hasn't noticed: what do you do?

In between the half-day sessions there were tasks to do such as:

Over the next two days please could you monitor the beginnings and ends of any lessons you are in and indicate if, in your opinion, the beginnings and ends of lessons are well managed (it may not always be possible for students to line up at start of lesson, but a calm atmosphere should be established. At the ends of lessons students should be dismissed in an orderly way).

They also worked in teams to produce induction booklets for new staff undertaking specific roles.

Taking so many staff offsite on a school day was a logistical challenge. A few didn't want to go or felt that they shouldn't go – what would happen without them? On the first occasion they went to a hotel and after that they worked at the local teachers' centre. But being offsite was important – it raised their status and their absence made everyone else realise how important they were. One said, 'The school stood still.'

Impact of the support staff project

The project leader was very focused and detailed every aspect of impact, with supporting evidence. There is now an established programme of CPD which offers options and choice: every Monday all staff have to opt for a workshop for their development. This means that the needs of all groups, including all the support staff groups, can be better addressed. Following more classroom-based support staff sessions, it was agreed that there needed to be induction programmes and packs in place for the various teams. These packs have included some of the confidence-raising strategies from the project's first phase to sustain development. A few support staff/teams ran twilight CPD sessions for others and offered sessions for future inclusion.

In evaluating the impact of this part of the project, there was a distinction made between products, processes and outcomes/impact for adults and pupils.

Products
Baseline: The same products were used for classroom-based support staff as for teachers, e.g. performance management forms, questionnaires around classroom practice, action plans and evaluations for CPD activities.

Impact: The school developed a number of pro-formas especially for classroom-based support staff. A questionnaire to measure progress was designed specifically for support staff and contained questions about how often and how confident they felt in, for example, giving verbal feedback to a teacher. The qualifications and experience audit and the personal action plan were designed to help support staff to identify needs and to make objectives clearer by asking them to specify success criteria and the support required to meet them. Support staff produced their own description of what makes a 'good lesson' and a 'good teacher', which was used with different groups in the second phase of the project. Another product was team induction policies. One technician said:

> It was a boost having time to get the induction policy written. It helped the team by refreshing people's understanding of what the job is. Resources are under better control and it's reinforced health and safety. We're more organised and now planning ahead.

Processes

While still involving support staff in whole-school processes, the school now provided opportunities for them to meet as a group and support each other, thus allowing them to contribute to whole-school improvement from their own perspective. They valued working separately from the teachers where they were able to express their views and realise that issues were often the same, despite working in different areas of the school. This allowed them the opportunity to find solutions in a safe and supportive environment.

Outcomes/Impact

Baseline: Information regarding the impact of support staff on teaching and learning was very anecdotal and disparate. Levels of confidence and understanding of their potential to make a difference varied significantly between different groups of support staff and individuals.

Impact: There was a clearer understanding of the influence support staff had on improving classroom practice. The activity to develop delivering difficult messages enabled support staff to tackle issues in a more proactive way – previously one admitted that she would have avoided raising them. Support staff had a better understanding of good lessons and teaching. A learning mentor considered that the heads of year (all support staff) had developed.

> They used to think it was all about shouting and now know that there are many ways of doing things and understand the need to work together to help the pupils.

Sharing some of their key perceptions about good lessons with the whole staff group helped to raise the status of support staff and highlighted their potential to make a positive difference in the classroom. Some learning mentors were now leading twilight sessions in understanding anger for other staff, including teachers.

A science technicians' group leader found the project useful in many ways, including raising career aspirations:

> We were a very insular team so it helped integrate us with others in the school. The Biology technician has gained much more confidence and is now going to do a PGCE; another wants to become a cover supervisor. One technician is doing science demonstrations, and the students look to her as a teacher. The students treat support staff with more respect.

B. Early professional development (EPD)

The second aspect of the project, which also ran over the two phases, concerned EPD. At the outset of the project, there were no specific processes for recently qualified teachers (RQTs), so any impact of existing support networks would not have been evaluated separately.

In 2007–8, ten teachers in their second, third and fourth years worked together and produced a guidance booklet for teachers in their second year. In 2008–9 six second-year teachers focused on identifying the criteria for outstanding lessons. They worked together for two days with the CPD leader offsite on what makes an outstanding lesson. Between the two sessions they did two observations of each other and each chose a day's external CPD opportunity. The project leader said, 'To go on a course is a treat, as normally the only courses people go on are ones run by exam boards.' Each person made a presentation to the rest of the group to disseminate their learning. They planned two development sessions for other staff on teaching outstanding lessons which they led themselves. Here is one of them:

TOP 10 TEACHING AND LEARNING TIPS FOR OUTSTANDING LESSONS
Presenting 'A QUEER FLOP'

1. ASSESSMENT... A range of methods employed by students and teachers
2. QUESTIONS... which challenge and develop thinking
3. an UNUSUAL... or creative element, the 'WOW or 'X-FACTOR'
4. ENGAGEMENT... and involvement of all students
5. an ENVIRONMENT... for learning that is secure... risk-taking and mistakes are encouraged

6. a RANGE... of teaching and learning styles employed
7. FUN... and enthusiasm from both teachers and students
8. LEARNING... achieved by all students
9. OBJECTIVES... that are clear and link to learning
10. PLANNING... of time, resources, structure that is efficient.

A range of CPD activities were undertaken, including coaching, peer observations and feedback, providing time for reflection, enabling contributions from all staff and group collaboration.

Impact of the EPD project

The EPD project was deemed to be successful, and again the project leader gave evidence of the impact on products, processes and outcomes on staff and pupils.

Products

A support pack was produced for RQTs which included 20 handy hints, EPD opportunities, information on the school-based MA and guidance on how to make a good lesson outstanding.

Processes

The school had established the need for this group of staff to meet together to share experiences and solutions, to highlight existing opportunities for their professional development and to be more proactive in taking advantage of them. Discussion of the pressures on RQTs led to suggestions for how senior leaders could encourage teachers to stay in the profession.

Outcomes/Impact

The teachers appreciated being listened to and supported in carrying through their action plans. One said, 'I like the feeling that I have been listened to and that my ideas are being put forward'; another said, 'It is helpful to know that I am experiencing similar barriers as others.'

A modern languages teacher considered that her questioning had improved and that the memory techniques she learned from other RQTs were having a marked impact.

> I'm getting pupils to think of questions. They are peer teaching. Pupils are enjoying Spanish more, they learn vocab more easily. The speaking module for GCSE shows improved results.

The whole *Effective Practices in CPD* project also had a significant impact upon the CPD leader. She felt that she now listened more and was offering more diverse CPD options and letting more people lead them. For instance, learning mentors led a session on social awareness and understanding each other's backgrounds which 12 people attended (seven support staff and five teachers). She understood the needs of support staff more:

> *The needs of teachers are much easier to address. Support staff were far less likely to come to me – I need to go more than half-way to find out what their needs are.*

It had helped her understand the importance of people having choice in their development activities. She summed this up by saying:

> *We empower people now and they ask far more. They have greater confidence to talk to me, pupils and teachers.*

She is, however, concerned that expectations have been raised. The next challenge was to meet those expectations within the school budget:

> *My challenge is to sustain development without the funding and the imperative of time pressures.*

The school intended to continue holding specific sessions for second year teachers and support staff to build on the project's work. A team-building exercise with the whole staff at an activity centre was planned for a professional development day. This was in response to a request from support staff.

Overall judgement on the project's success

Both parts of the project were very successful. Crucially, the school embedded and consolidated learning from the first year of the project and developed it in the second. The results of the questionnaire (see Appendix) in the first year of the project, which compared adult and students' perceptions of progress over time, showed that the adults' perception was that 16 of the good practices described were occurring more often than previously, with two occurring the same number of times. However, student perception was that just four of the good practices described were occurring more often, 13 less often and one the same number of times. The evidence uncovered through the questionnaire gave clarity to the focus of the specific work to be undertaken.

Features of effective professional development

In considering features of effective professional development, these were definitely in place:

- The importance of engaging with a variety of CPD opportunities.
- The value of time for reflection and feedback.
- The significance of collaborative CPD: participants in both projects valued learning from each other rather than from senior staff or external experts.
- The importance of strategic leadership of CPD: the staff development leader was very strategic but admitted she found that managing a project was a challenge:

  It's easy to get overwhelmed with the budget and invoicing rather than spending time on the important things.

- The need for clarity of purpose at the outset in CPD activity: the project director and all staff interviewed were clear about what their purpose was.
- The value of a specific focus and goal for CPD activity, aligned to clear timescales: although this was the case for this project some activities were planned for the whole school year, i.e. after the project deadline.
- Participants' ownership of CPD activity: the support staff in particular felt ownership and led sessions for each other and teachers.
- Understanding how to evaluate the impact of CPD: the project leader was wary of quantitative data and questionnaires but had now used them with success, valuing the way the evidence helped her to focus on the appropriate next steps (see Appendix).
- Including a focus on pupil outcomes: there could have been even more of a focus upon pupil outcomes but the project's aim was to affect staff first and foremost, and future evaluative work can focus on whether there is an impact upon pupils. There was already some evidence, e.g. in the Spanish GCSE speaking module, that results had improved.

The project leader considered that 'Best value was achieved by taking groups of staff out of school to reflect, discuss and develop new skills.' There would have been value in considering whether there was any resulting disruption to pupil learning and well-being. Perhaps better use of professional development days could have been made instead of the school deciding to convert some whole days into twilight sessions. Nevertheless this was a very successful project which achieved much.

Appendix

Results of questionnaire

		Students			Staff		
		June 2007	June 2008	Diff	June 2007	June 2008	Diff
1	Lessons begin with the teacher stating the learning objectives.	3.1	2.9	-0.2	3.2	3.5	0.3
2	Learning objectives help students understand what they need to learn.	3.1	2.8	-0.3	3.2	3.4	0.2
3	The teacher tells students what they are looking for in order for the students to succeed in the lesson.	2.8	2.4	-0.4	3.1	3.1	0
4	The teacher's verbal comments help students to improve.	2.8	2.9	0.1	3.3	3.5	0.2
5	When teachers mark books, comments are linked to improvement.	3	2.7	-0.3	3.1	3.3	0.2
6	Peer and self-assessment happens.	2.9	2.6	-0.3	2.8	3.1	0.3
7	Results in tests and homework are discussed with students.	2.5	2.4	-0.1	2.9	3.1	0.2
8	Teachers ask questions that make students think about their learning.	2.7	2.5	-0.2	2.7	2.8	0.1
9	The teacher tells students how the work they are doing could be useful in other lessons.	2	2.1	0.1	2.2	2.4	0.2
10	The teacher OCCASIONALLY tells students how the work they are doing could be useful outside of school.	1.9	2	0.1	2.3	2.5	0.2
11	Students are asked to work in pairs or groups.	3	2.9	-0.1	3.4	3.5	0.1

12	Working in pairs and groups helps students understand the work more fully.	3.1	3	-0.1	2.9	3.1	0.2
13	Teachers try to involve everyone in the lesson.	2.7	2.6	-0.1	3.3	3.6	0.3
14	Most students feel happy to contribute in lessons.	3	3	0	2.8	2.9	0.1
15	Teachers go over what has been learnt at the end of the lesson.	2.1	2.2	0.1	2.8	2.9	0.1
16	Most students know what level/ grade they are working on in lessons.	2.6	2.5	-0.1	2.8	2.8	0
17	Some students know their target level/grade in each subject.	2.6	2.5	-0.1	2.8	3.1	0.3
18	Knowing target levels/grades helps students to improve.	3.2	3	-0.2	2.6	2.9	0.3

The questionnaire was completed in JUNE 2007 by 52 staff and 89 students from Years 8, 9, 10 and 12.

The questionnaire was completed in JUNE 2008 by 51 staff and 88 students from Years 8, 9, 10 and 12.

Responses were given values from 4: strongly agree/often, to 1: disagree/ never.

An overall response of 3 or above is quite positive and highlighted in dark grey.

An overall response below 2 is quite negative and highlighted in black.

The difference in scores has been calculated for adults and students separately.

Adults' perception is that 16 of the good practices described are occurring more often now than a year ago, with two occurring the same number of times.

Students' perception is that four of the good practices described are occurring more often, 13 less often and one the same number of times.

Individuals' comments were also added, but these have not been included in the Appendix.

Chapter 10

DIY CPD: a system for professional learning for all staff

Steve Lloyd

Context

The project was based in a large community first school with an age range of 5–9, with 400 pupils on the roll. The vast majority of pupils are of white British heritage and virtually all have English as their first language. The proportion of pupils with learning difficulties and/or disabilities is broadly average. An integral part of the school is a speech and language unit with places for 18 pupils with statements detailing their particular needs. Children begin school in September in the year in which they are 5, initially part time. They start in one of the three parallel Reception classes which constitute part of the Early Years Foundation Stage (EYFS). All children have attended some kind of pre-school setting. The school holds a number of awards, including Healthy School, Activemark and Rights Respecting Schools. A private provider manages day care and an after-school club on the school premises. The school is one of ten first schools serving a large rural town.

Prior to this project, CPD opportunities tended to be what was on offer through the local authority and other local providers. In the main, CPD opportunities were reactive and externally delivered and there was no plan for the deployment of this resource, although there had been attempts to match school and individuals' requests according to the school's identified priorities. The school had staff who had benefited from opportunities offered through the local authority or by the (then) National College for School Leadership (NCSL), with the lessons learned through these activities disseminated across the school in an ad hoc manner. Other than statutory requirements, such as Health and Safety training, CPD opportunities were entirely focused on the needs of teaching staff. Consequently, CPD practice lacked any strategic management or leadership, and, therefore, impact was neither planned for nor evaluated.

This project was initially led by a new headteacher, but over the period of both phases of the project, leadership was transferred to a key member of the school staff.

The headteacher firmly believed that the school had:

All the skills and knowledge we required to be 'outstanding' within the staff we already had, we just didn't have the mechanism to get that information from where it was to where it was needed.

Phase 1 project

The lack of any CPD policy resulted in a serendipitous approach that worked for some staff but not for others. The learning needs of staff were identified during performance management meetings. In most cases meeting these needs depended on the availability and costs of external courses. The budget-setting cycle and the CPD cycle following performance management were not synchronised, which resulted in additional pressures on supply cover budgets or non-availability of courses. The school relied wholly on external input as part of its planned CPD.

This baseline practice had a negative impact on the culture of the school, shown through a lack of clear self-knowledge of the skills required for effective practice in the classroom. This was equally the case for both teachers and teaching assistants. There was no framework against which any member of staff could judge their own or others' performance and no common understanding of what a framework might contain. This absence of a common understanding meant that CPD opportunities were not personalised. This led to many colleagues believing that any attempt to engender change through classroom observation and feedback was perceived as a negative process, irrespective of their own existing skills, knowledge or capabilities.

Aim

The key aim of the first phase of the project was to create a professional development framework to which all staff could subscribe, and use, to evaluate performance and identify areas of future development. It was intended to engage teachers and teaching assistants in classroom-based 'change' projects based on needs identified by the published National Professional Standards.

The main areas of focus were on:

1. links between teachers' Professional Standards and performance
2. the planning processes

3. models of support and challenge.

The main process used to implement these changes was through the formation of a self-selected 'change' team which represented staff at all levels of experience and included TAs, teachers and senior leadership team. Through the funding available in this project, this team has had the time to meet, think, write, plan and reflect as part of their own development. These were often whole-day sessions, with occasional external input on coaching and mentoring, and a 'critical friend' from a local higher education institution.

This developed a more open and honest culture, which allowed issues such as status and hierarchy to be challenged and developed. These staff, when interviewed, identified the impact upon their own thinking as follows:

- *The mixed team has broken down barriers.*
- *It was an opportunity to experience coaching and mentoring.*
- *It provided the opportunity to contribute and reflect on their own practice.*
- *It developed open, honest relationships in a professional context.*
- *We found ourselves talking in the most open and honest way about issues that can be 'taboo' in the general day-to-day life of the school.*

The key aims of this group were to ensure that:

1. the teacher and TA Standards were more accessible, useful and usable
2. elements of the Standards were exemplified to allow staff to make judgements and identify areas of progression for themselves
3. peer coaching and mentoring were the processes that would be used to support development and progression.

Impact of phase 1

At this stage it was very difficult to identify any real impact across the school. The change team identified the impact on themselves through this vision statement:

By being focused, open and honest, and with real support, we can progress to greater knowledge and better practice.

Individuals reflected on the importance of certain elements of their practice, including: a recognition of the importance of keeping reflective journals; the use of a 'critical friend' to challenge and support the process; a greater awareness of the complementary roles of teacher and teaching assistant; the relevance of the 'Standards'. There was a key desire to develop their own practices across the whole staff in phase 2 of the project.

Phase 2 project

Having completed the first phase of testing out an idea for DIY CPD with a representative working party, they developed a whole-school approach.

Aim

This was intended to embed and consolidate the learning of phase 1 through the use of self-evaluation tools based on the National Standards for teachers and TAs to support professional reflection and help develop practice.

The working party obtained baseline evidence of the needs identified in phase 1.

- Lesson observations as part of the performance management process had identified over-reliance on 'teacher talk', and very little evidence of assessment for learning (AfL) practice.
- Subject and team leaders had identified a need to develop more challenge in activities to differentiate work for more able children.
- Informal audits of weak areas in children's learning led to a desire to 'narrow the gap' in achievement between some targeted children and their peers.

The plan was to take a number of approaches to address these needs and embed the use of the tools, namely:

Big picture events – key staff meetings to introduce the rationale, purposes and systems for DIY CPD activity. Where possible a number of different members of the working group planned and led these events.

Joint focused planning (JFP) enquiry – a number of paired activities based around AfL activities with peer planning and reflection on new approaches to AfL, through classroom observation and feedback.

Funded research bursaries – all staff were given the opportunity to bid for one of three bursaries with a focus on 'narrowing the gap'.

Professional challenge for TAs – opportunities to take charge of learning activities in classes releasing class teachers.

High-quality cover – planned extension activities with external providers and key internal 'experts' to involve classes in 'Arts'-focused activity releasing teachers for CPD activities.

Coaching skills acquisition – development opportunities for all staff in coaching and for some TAs in leading cover lessons.

Coaching – used as an integral part of the development of all staff, particularly following any developmental activity.

Impact of phase 2

The working group was very aware of the need to change the culture of the staff to move from a 'laissez-faire' approach to CPD to one that was more focused on the twin aims of raising teacher and TA professional standards and to impact positively upon pupils' achievement and attainment.

In order to do this they recognised that a holistic approach was necessary which empowered individuals to make their own choices about their professional development with the support of peers and the CPD leader as 'coach'.

They took a pragmatic view to overcome the teachers' sensibilities about being out of the classroom for CPD activities by raising the skill levels of the TAs to lead in the key areas of numeracy and arts. This in itself provided useful professional development for those TAs involved. Every one of the approaches used in the CPD project also had an element of peer/team responsibility which ensured a higher commitment than there otherwise might have been and offered increased ownership.

In terms of provision of new CPD opportunities there was little that could have been improved. Impact evaluation, however, was difficult due to the project timescales, which meant that any attainment data were collected over a relatively short period of time. Triangulation of staff perceptions, the 'critical friend' and lesson observations told a significant part of the story, but little quantitative data were evident. The school, however, saw the development of attitudinal surveys with children as a significant next step as they sought to embed this approach further.

Overall judgement on the project's success

Staff engagement and involvement in the project was high, with all teaching staff being involved to some degree. Most TAs led at least one lesson over the period of the project, with a particular focus on Maths. All teachers worked in pairs to plan, teach and be observed by each other at least twice. Each pair of teachers had two coaching sessions and peer reflection time. The lesson areas (focusing on AfL strategies) took place in a range of contexts, including Maths, phonics, note-taking, handwriting and PE. Each pair of teachers recorded and reported their key findings.

The *Effective Practices in CPD* project enabled the school to move forward significantly to alter not only the style of CPD provision but also to address some of the underlying cultural 'us and them' issues that can exist when there are attempts to link CPD provision with performance management structures, such as lesson observation and the Professional Standards. The introduction of peer supportive structures and coaching built on the statutory expectations of performance management and demonstrably moved the school from 'good' to 'outstanding', clearly evidenced by the extracts from a variety of reports below.

In February 2009 Ofsted reported the following:

> *Considerable improvements in the past two years to the EYFS provision have built on the satisfactory profile noted in the last report. Consequently, children are now making excellent progress in Reception. This has yet to have a full impact on attainment in Years 1 and 2 but, nevertheless, standards at the end of Year 2 are average and rising, with pupils achieving well.*

Local authority validation of self-evaluation form evidence in January 2009 stated:

> *There is greater coherence in the school's systems for evaluating its performance and needs and the way it responds to those findings.*

The members of staff reported that they had developed greater self-confidence and a wider range of skills as a result of the *Effective Practices in CPD* project. The culture of the school had improved; for example, there was an improved feeling of teamwork as members of staff had developed a greater understanding and appreciation of each other's roles. Pupils were showing a different attitude to the adults they worked with, regarding teachers, TAs and others as people who can and do help them with their learning.

The 'critical friend' commented on the project outcomes in March 2009:

It is significant that the principles and processes that are being used by professionals to develop their work are the same or parallel to the principles and processes that they want the children to experience.

In the same way that children need to feel secure, that they belong, that they are helping others and can have help when they need it, we need support as professionals. It is an important question for the school to address: how can time and resources be directed towards 'supervision', i.e. a periodic formal opportunity to take stock and reflect with someone whose role is to affirm, challenge and share ways forward.

The latter should be achieved through the school's arrangements for performance management.

Features of effective professional development

In considering features of effective professional development, the following were definitely in place:

- Establishing clarity of purpose at the outset in CPD activity

The project leader and all staff interviewed were clear about the focus of the project and its potential impact.

- Specifying a focus and goal for CPD activity aligned to clear timescales

These were evident but the overall timescales for the project did not fit comfortably with the planning cycle of the school year.

- Including a focus on pupil outcomes in CPD activity

This would need to be the next strategic aim.

- Ensuring participants' ownership of CPD activity

All staff, the headteacher, project leader, teachers and support staff felt that they had been empowered within an overarching framework to take control of their own CPD.

- Engaging with a variety of CPD opportunities
- Including time for reflection and feedback, including paired activities

- Ensuring collaborative approaches to CPD

Participants in both projects valued learning from and with each other as well as from senior staff or external experts.

- Developing strategic leadership of CPD

The CPD leader became more strategic as the headteacher delegated more as the project developed.

- Understanding how to evaluate the impact of CPD

From the start of phase 2, impact measures had been considered and the use of triangulation of data was developed with support from the critical friend.

The team set themselves their own success criteria to enable them to have some measure of the impact of each of the strands of this project. These addressed not only the basic criteria relating to the project's success but also attempted to gauge some measure of the more cultural elements. In each case the project leader trialled ways to gather and triangulate evidence to try to show what impact the various elements of the phase 2 project had achieved. These included lesson observations, teacher reflective journals, internal pupil attainment data, Ofsted and LA reports, coaching and performance management pro-formas and reports, diaries and project reports, and structured interviews. There has been obvious improvement in the project leaders' understanding of the process of impact evaluation and their next steps would require further exploration of how to gauge the impact upon the practice of colleagues involved and then the impact of this upon pupils' learning. The *Effective Practices in CPD* work has built an excellent platform for this further development.

An abridged version of impact with the related evidence base can be seen in Table 10.1.

Table 10.1: Impact expected and achieved

Focus	Impact expected	Impact achieved
Full staff entitlement	High take-up of both joint focused planning (JFP) and bursary opportunities	14 out of 16 colleagues took part in the JFP project.
Assessment for learning (AfL)	Teachers would commit to the school's chosen AfL focus	*It has been very nice to be able to have time to work with a colleague without feeling the pressure of having one more thing to do. It has been good to focus on AfL and has been an opportunity to reflect on the AfL that goes on in my classroom.*
	Adults would probe children's learning using a variety of AfL strategies	*I think that it was a good idea to show these possible Level 5 students the big picture – their target level – and they were able to plan their next steps with support. So I think this gives them a clear focus and improves their ability to plan for their own learning.* And *Generally this group found it harder to talk together and verbalise the success criteria but by the end they realised that they needed to learn the division facts for the multiplication tables. I asked them what would help them to do this and ideas included daily practice and a visual display.*
Teaching assistants	TAs feel more empowered	Thirteen TAs signed up to do Maths cover, 10 TAs took responsibility for leading Maths lessons, five TAs either led or co-led one of the three bursary awards. Two TAs remarked: *I really enjoyed doing the Maths lessons in different year groups, and the drumming club bursary.* *I never thought it would give me the confidence to offer to lead an after-school drama club.*

Teachers	Apply new-found ideas in their future teaching	Lesson observations show that the use of 'phonic friends' continued after the research period.
	Be more open to learn in a collaborative way	Teachers enjoyed working with a partner for hour-long teaching/ planning sessions: *It was good to work collaboratively with my partner and share ideas. It was non-judgmental.*
Greater clarity as to what has been learned	Coaching would facilitate further learning for TAs and teachers	As a response to the coaching sessions and the high visibility of the phase 2 CPD project, the leader of the Speech and Language Unit asked the CPD leader to conduct a team coaching session to help them *'resolve a problem'.*
	Teachers observe peers to support learning	Observers filming lessons gave more valuable feedback than traditional approaches.
	Improved practice	*Looking back on my practice I have asked children to answer questions without giving them sufficient time to think about an answer. I realise now this does not help their learning and that time needs to be given for thinking time.*

Chapter 11

Growing together: leadership of learning in a local authority

John Tandy

Context

Primary headteachers in this local authority have a tradition of networking and meeting regularly: partnership with the Borough is strong. Headteachers' networks have historically tended to be location based within the local authority. At the beginning of the project, the primary school heads came together to work with the LA and to be a source of capacity for the development and evaluation of professional learning across the Borough. The Director of Children's Services had asked the Headteachers' Group to develop jointly a Leadership Charter that was a summary of effective leadership practice in the Borough.

This project had a significant impact upon the thinking and practice of participants and influenced networking and collaborative practice among primary headteachers across a local authority.

Phase 1 project

Before the project, the Borough, together with the leaders of the heads' network, tended to develop CPD opportunities that were focused around traditional delivery methods involving out-of-school events and conferences. This provided an opportunity for colleagues to work together: all sessions were focused around key professional imperatives that were based around national issues. Opportunities offered to school leaders traditionally comprised opportunities to coach and be coached by other experienced professionals, induction arrangements for new headteachers, brokerage of programmes beyond the LA and also locally designed offerings within the Borough.

Participation was founded on an individual's willingness to learn and their school's capacity to enable the learning to take place. There was a sense that colleagues would leave their workspace to gather information *about* key and emerging areas of practice rather than *engage with* them. There was little attempt to garner any understanding of what the participants required and how they would prefer to learn, and an unclear understanding of tools that facilitated this. The evaluation of CPD was always completed using a LA printed form that gauged participant reaction and response to learning opportunities rather than learning itself. The partnerships were generally activity- and delivery-oriented and had little focus on, or mechanisms for, establishing the learning and development that occurred.

Aims

The project was set up for a group of up to 21 primary headteachers to work together to explore enquiry-based methods of evaluating the impact of professional development and communities of practice.

More specifically, the project aimed to enable participants to:

- enquire into existing good practice in the LA
- explore other models of effective leadership of learning
- commit to sharing practice across schools
- accelerate the building of leadership capacity at all levels
- begin to establish strategies for succession planning in the LA
- contribute to the development of a Leadership Charter.

An external consultant was employed to manage and to lead meetings, workshops and conferences. The project was rooted in the context of the Borough and was constructed to be sustained over time, enquiry focused, personalised, collaborative and to link with participants' priorities.

The project was structured around three core processes: collaborative enquiry, models of leadership and community of practice.

- Collaborative enquiry: Participants were involved in enquiry into their own and others' leadership practice.
- Models of leadership: Participants explored, shared and documented practice to serve as a local model of leadership practice in the LA.
- Community of practice: Participants worked together and made use of enquiry, group facilitation and peer coaching and were committed to collaborative working.

Collaborative enquiry

A system of enquiry walks ran in parallel with the joint working sessions. Participants worked in groups of three, each of whom tended not to have had previous experience of working collaboratively with the others. Each participant chose an aspect of their school that they were proud of and invited a group of colleagues and a facilitator to visit their school and to take part in an enquiry walk. This comprised a question formulated by the host headteacher to guide the work of the visiting observers; their brief was to consider how the chosen focus permeated the work of their school and to note (usually on post-its) what they saw, felt and could hear that was relevant to the chosen theme, when talking to children and to staff, visiting classrooms and observing the work of the school generally. The enquiry walk took place in the morning session and a summary report was assembled and written during the afternoon, providing immediate feedback.

Models of leadership and community of practice

Joint working sessions – day meetings, residential conferences – were practical sessions during which a range of techniques were used to draw out good working practice from participants and to inject new ideas drawn from current thinking about leadership, underpinned by opportunities to reflect on learning. Protocols to ensure confidentiality and to build trust between participants were agreed. The principle was to *engage with* rather than *learn about* good practice. Each session was designed to appeal to a range of learning styles, using, for example, photographs, fish bowl, check-ins, marketplace, activities to challenge and develop thinking and understanding of participants. Participants greatly valued this 'active learning' approach which they described as inspirational and a key part of the project. They welcomed the opportunity to engage in activities that were participative and depended on them reacting to and considering the implications of stimulus materials. When they worked in small groups, there was some physical involvement; for example, as they were grouped and regrouped, they moved around the room and reported to other groups, which reinforced active approaches. On one occasion participants were asked to complete discussions as they walked together outdoors. They contrasted these approaches with more passive ways of working that were the norm in many CPD activities they had previously experienced.

The first phase of the project concluded with a conference to celebrate outcomes and to begin to involve the headteachers who had not taken part in the project. The agenda was agreed between project headteachers and the LA. There was a focus on active approaches to learning.

Phase 2 project

The funding for the second phase of the project gave the group the opportunity to consolidate and extend their understanding of professional learning, and how it might be facilitated and designed through extending the work of the network. The funding was felt to be a 'huge bonus'.

They developed wider engagement in the work of the network and facilitated expanded networks. In addition to the Leadership Learning Charter that the group had developed, they also wished to formalise their learning by creating a resource that could be used by leaders across the authority.

A number of new tools and strategies were developed to facilitate powerful professional dialogue and reflection and school-based collaborative enquiry. The network developed a process through which 'enquiry walks' were used to complete these essential tasks. This process involved:

- establishing a school-determined enquiry question that is explicitly linked to an area of recent improvement and learning
- establishing, agreeing and communicating the process and protocol for all involved
- exploring the school context and focus
- engaging with practice – including lesson observation, scrutiny of student work, conversation with staff, immersion in the learning environment
- gathering and recording collaborative analysis of data
- writing reports
- engaging others in the enquiry and generating next steps.

Participants developed a school-based enquiry programme that enabled an aspect of a school or a particular theme of professional learning to be viewed and evaluated in practice. Learning from completed 'enquiry walks' has fed directly into the Leadership Learning Charter.

Impact of the projects

It's like a runaway train… you can't stop it... it has its own momentum.
(LA co-leader)

The most powerful piece of CPD I have ever done.
(Headteacher)

The enquiry walks and the collaborative working contributed to the Leadership Learning Charter that was now in its final draft form. Participants believed that it encapsulated key principles of effective leadership within the LA. However, it was felt that the true impact and value of the project was to be found in the professional learning of participants and, most significantly, in approaches to CPD practices and professional learning of participants and colleagues across the local authority.

As the project evolved, the Charter (product) became a secondary focus as participants realised the power of enquiry walks (process). In evaluations, participants felt empowered and confident enough to address a whole range of issues with colleagues. The collegiate approach of the project has strengthened collaborative working, while simultaneously strengthening participants' autonomy.

Participants were now using active learning approaches to CPD in their own schools, drawing on materials and practices they used and experienced in the project: participating in the project and experiencing successful collaborative learning had influenced the way in which the headteacher of a primary school led CPD in her school. Protocols that drew on those used during the headteachers' work were agreed to ensure that collaborative working was non-judgemental, mutually supportive and nurturing but also challenging. CPD now incorporated active learning approaches and reflection, and the use of trios when appropriate. This was said to have resulted in more effective and engaged working practices. The local authority had changed its practice relating to courses that it organised for practitioners:

- Courses were better described, objectives were clearer and the immediate evaluation forms had been redesigned to be more meaningful.
- The conferences at the conclusion of the two phases of the project were organised more collaboratively and resulted in recognition of the importance of participants' input to planning: the LA had traditionally taken the lead in leading and organising primary headteachers' conferences.
- Via their network meetings, practitioners in turn felt able to draw on their own knowledge and familiarity with their strengths and areas for development in order to inform the content and design of CPD opportunities. This was a significant change in LA practice.

The enquiry walk model had a significant impact upon all members of the group, which led to changes in CPD practice in other work with headteachers and other groups in the LA. The impact had arisen from schools drawing on the feedback and conclusions of the enquiries and also from the learning of the enquiry teams.

> *We have been given the confidence to draw on the wealth of our own expertise… to find answers from within as well as from research.*
>
> (Headteacher)

One head of a school in a relatively affluent catchment area took part in an enquiry walk at a school in a more deprived area. She had since drawn on their practice to introduce a new logging system for recording information about vulnerable children in her own school and felt (she provided no evidence) that this was enabling her to address part of the 'Be safe' Every Child Matters outcome more effectively.

One primary school chose to focus on 'developing the positive behaviour of children'. Their enquiry question was:

> *How do the strategies put in place to support children in making positive decisions about their behaviour impact upon the climate for learning in the school?*

The headteacher had briefed staff in advance about the purpose of the enquiry to ensure its positive nature was understood. The school found the resulting feedback affirmative and it quantified how the enquiry focus was a strength of the school.

This school's headteacher took part in an enquiry walk at another primary school; the focus was on active learning. He was inspired and informed by practice at the school and used observed practice to challenge teaching practices in his school. Maths was the first curriculum area that was addressed during 2007–8: he believed that changes to practice informed by this enquiry walk contributed to improved KS2 Maths results in 2008 – well above the national average and representing significant added value. The observed active learning approaches were used by staff to develop practice at the head's school. Pupils who had been reluctant to engage with learning were 'drawn into' their Maths work and, as the attainment data showed, their learning had improved as a result.

The head commented:

> *It is early days yet but the progress tracking figures that I have would indicate a steadily improving picture. The picture is not perfect but does show an improving picture. It must be noted that the age-appropriate expectations move up during the year, and from July to September.*

He felt that the structure of the enquiry walk was focused and enabled a wealth of minutiae to be included, resulting in a report that captures 'real' practice at the school. This was in contrast with 'learning walks' that were less focused and less directed. Sharing of the school's enquiry had resulted in a group of headteachers from another authority visiting his school to enquire about good practice at the school.

Another primary school chose to focus on how Every Child Matters outcomes were integrated into the work of the school. The distinction between Ofsted inspection and the enquiry walks was thrown into sharp focus as an Ofsted inspection (resulting in 'an outstanding school' commendation) had taken place during the preceding week. The enquiry walk was *appreciative enquiry* and its way of working helped to make staff feel confident as it progressed. It was felt to be 'appreciative' in the sense that what was shared was valued by the enquirers, who were not felt to be judgemental. The affirmatory and celebratory tone of the enquiry walk gave staff a boost in a way that LA and Ofsted visits did not.

Following the walk, the school had implemented one of the report's recommendations by providing opportunities for staff to work more closely and collaboratively to use the expertise of a colleague in PSHE and Citizenship. Planning was now completed collaboratively and team teaching had enabled the 'expert' teacher to influence the practice of colleagues, e.g. by working alongside each other in classrooms.

The successful experiences of schools during phase 1 led to further enquiry walks taking place during the second phase of the project: this in turn led to a ripple effect that permeated thinking and practice across the LA, actively and deliberately promoted by members of the Learn Together group. This CPD strategy was being embedded in the collaborative work of schools.

Another headteacher linked implementation of professional learning with the school meeting Ofsted expectations: 'I feel that many of the ideas of good practice I chose to adopt helped our school achieve an "outstanding" Ofsted report.' She commented on the positive attitudes towards professional development of her staff, due to the affirmatory ethos of the enquiry walk:

> I have used the report as part of my performance management interviews this week and my staff feel very proud of their achievements. Because they are now so used to having visitors sharing their practice – when I suggest we put ourselves forward for external training projects like 'Every Child a Writer' I get a resounding 'yes' rather than a 'What's in it for me?'. To conclude, the whole experience has… given my staff a chance to shine in a non-threatening environment.

The project had also influenced the design, for example, of headteacher mentoring practice, Leadership Pathways working and Preparation for Middle Leadership CPD in the LA: active learning was now incorporated into the CPD design.

A deputy headteachers group representing 22 schools now used the enquiry walk CPD model; collaborative learning had become part of their practice. The headteachers group in another area had changed to work in a more collaborative way. There was greater sharing and collaborative working on common issues. The chair of the group was a member of the Learn Together group.

The headteacher cluster groups mostly included a member of the Learn Together group who were influencing their way of working. One cluster had reallocated the CPD budget to enable it to work in ways similar to those used in the project.

> *This way of working is more relevant than NCSL courses. It is always about school, children, reality and relationships rather than the theory of NCSL material.*
>
> (Primary headteacher)

The successful and positive experience of the Learn Together group have energised colleagues and was influencing practice across the Borough. The original headteacher group that comprised the Learn Together partnership was expanded and a new phase of working was planned to embed and enhance the successful practice developed in the project's two phases.

The project allowed participants to focus upon the drivers for professional learning and more carefully construct learning opportunities that matched the context of learners' practice and the learning needs of the professionals involved. The network had become larger in scale and participation in networks was greater and more meaningful.

The nature of the learning changed within the work of the network. The expectation of participants was that their learning was:

- connected to their practice and their learning needs
- sustained over time
- collaborative – with opportunities for facilitated and structured encounters with one another's practice
- real work focused – 'we have used the maxim that "learning is the work" consciously and explicitly throughout the design of the project'
- reflective
- personalised.

Overall judgement on the project's success

The project was clearly very successful. It began with the need to develop a Leadership Charter that reflected effective leadership practice in the LA. This provided direction and purpose for the range of activities that led to its creation within a timescale that was clear but included some flexibility to anticipate unforeseen demands on headteachers' time. The range of CPD opportunities that proved to be so stimulating and exciting for participants was a key contributor to the success of the project. Reflection and collaborative working were inextricably linked to this. The project was led by an external consultant and facilitator whose work was greatly respected and valued by participants; part of the project's success was the way in which participants were enabled to embed and take responsibility for the development and enhancement of practice using skills, knowledge and understanding developed during the project. They clearly now had ownership of the outcomes.

Participants were fulsome in their praise of what took place; none had any criticism to make of the project itself. The views of participants are summarised in this comment by a participating headteacher:

> *The project would have been even better if we could have engaged in the process with all schools several years ago (and not had to limit it to a pilot) as the powerful impact is that all schools are now beginning to see the real value of enquiry-based learning as a firm basis for effective CPD and the raising of standards through learning from others and appreciative enquiry.*

Features of effective professional development

In this project the following features of effective professional development were in place:

- the need for clarity of purpose at the outset in CPD activity
- the value of a specific focus and goal for CPD activity, aligned to clear timescales
- the need to develop participants' ownership of CPD activity
- the importance of engaging with a variety of CPD opportunities
- the value of time for reflection and feedback
- the significance of collaborative CPD
- the importance of strategic leadership of CPD.

The project might have been even more successful if the following had been considered more:

- Including a focus on pupil outcomes in CPD activity

A focus on pupil outcomes was implicit in the project with improvements to pupil learning expected to result from the enquiry walk findings and working as a leader within the effective practice summarised in the Leadership Charter. However, improved pupil outcomes were not explicit in the project design.

Enhancing pupils' learning was always a core aim for the headteachers who felt that this project was about enabling and equipping them to do so more effectively. The next stage would be to evaluate whether the leadership and learning behaviours within this project had brought about gains in pupil learning that could be evidenced.

- Understanding how to evaluate the impact of CPD

This project had a product – the Leadership Charter – and processes – collaborative enquiry and leadership learning – as its objectives. Completing the document and engaging in enquiry was an end point for participants who were sharing the successes of what was being achieved as they implemented their professional learning in their schools. But this was serendipitous: more systematic evaluation was not part of the original design of the project. There was more celebration than systematic evaluation, which would facilitate any necessary refinement and identification of the next steps in development.

Part 3

Concluding comments

Chapter 12

Conclusion

Vivienne Porritt and Peter Earley

- Main findings from the case studies
- Impact evaluation
- Ways forward

In this concluding chapter we consider the lessons learned from the TDA *Effective Practices in CPD* project and, in particular, highlight why effective CPD matters, as shown by the case studies which concluded the project. We begin by considering the importance of language and the terms used for CPD, before outlining the nine approaches which the overall project's findings suggest are crucial to effective CPD. Other main findings from the case studies discussed in this chapter include the use of time, coaching, and embedding learning to achieve change. Another valuable lesson learned from the project is the importance of evaluating the impact of CPD and, building on our discussion in Chapter 1, this is considered in relation to establishing a baseline and impact picture, and understanding evidence sources and asserted or substantiated evidence.

In the last section of this final chapter – 'Ways forward' – we consider the project's main findings and the lessons to be learned in the light of the TDA's new *Professional Development Strategy for the Children's Workforce in Schools, 2009–12*, launched in 2009. We emphasise that the lessons learned from the case study schools are significant in ensuring that professional development continues to make a difference to the learning of our colleagues and, significantly, to that of children and young people.

Main findings from the case studies

Language matters

A notable outcome of the *Effective Practices in CPD* project was real culture change within involved organisations, irrespective of the initial starting point and practice within these organisations. In the first chapter, we emphasised what we mean by CPD and why it matters. In exploring such questions through the *Effective Practices in CPD* projects, a very wide continuum of knowledge and understanding about this emerged. One of the aspects that showed the greatest variety was the language used by different organisations around CPD. Tensions of language reflect the cultural transitions around the CPD practice highlighted in the case studies. The case studies reflect our preferred language in this field: it is worth, however, noting the range of terminology in use.

There is still widespread use of the word '*Inset*'. It means 'In-service education and training' and was first introduced over 25 years ago by means of the INSET grant to schools which was used to send teachers on courses. This word reflects schools that do not exist anymore and needs to be consigned to history. The most fascinating use of this word we came across is 'Inset CPD sessions' – this is either a belt-and-braces approach or it reflects some of the schizophrenic thinking that still exists around continuing professional development.

We also acknowledge the importance of describing the leadership of CPD as a key role, one that is held by a senior leader who is a member of the school's leadership team and who is supported by a team of other colleagues with responsibility in this area, such as induction tutors, school business managers, higher level teaching assistants (HLTAs) and middle leaders. The role is varyingly described as CPD coordinator, staff development coordinator, training manager and still, far too often, Inset coordinator. We need to make a determined effort to shift the language from the use of 'Inset' to 'CPD' and 'coordinator' to 'leader' to reflect the value of strategic leadership of this important area.

Other words used throughout the *Effective Practices in CPD* project suggest predominant perceptions about ways of working. What do the words '*provide*', '*deliver*', '*receive*', '*run*' and '*training*' suggest to you? For many colleagues in schools, this language reflects a mechanistic, transactional process that encourages passivity. Such words should be replaced with language that suggests a two-way process and which encourages involvement and active participation (see Table 12.1).

Table 12.1

Existing language	Changed language
provide/deliver	offer
receive	engage in
run a session	lead a session
training	learning and development
Inset	professional development
management/coordination	leadership

There are also debates about whether the phrase 'continuing professional development' excludes colleagues other than teachers, with suggestions that a better phrase would be 'school workforce development'. Alternatively, the term 'staff development' might be used which gives due emphasis to inclusivity, while avoiding any sensitivities around the word 'professional' (Bubb et al., 2009; Bubb and Earley, 2010). Our preference, like the TDA's, is to retain the phrase 'professional development' and to promote its inclusive use. All our colleagues in schools play a key role in supporting children and young people, and approach this work with a professional attitude that should attract the highest level of support and development. CPD leaders will want to decide which term is going to be best in their context to help to bring about any necessary cultural change.

If we do not yet have a shared language about CPD, it will come as no surprise that we are still working towards how to achieve effective professional development practice. The *Effective Practices in CPD* project reminds us of the journey we are still taking in moving towards systemic understanding and practice: we are pleased to have the opportunity to highlight lessons and successes on the way.

Effective CPD matters

In learning lessons from the case studies which the London Centre for Leadership in Learning (LCLL) conducted, we would also wish to emphasise that what makes a difference to colleagues, to schools, and to children and young people is how *effective* CPD activity actually is. According to the research syntheses from the Evidence for Policy and Practice Information and Co-ordinating Centre (EPPI) from 2003[1] onwards, CPD activity that is effective needs to incorporate, for example, reflection, collaborative approaches, external input and for such activity to be determined by individual needs and sustained over time. In phase 1, participants in many projects were learning or applying these lessons almost as if for the first time, so a key lesson may be the time it takes for schools and their leaders to implement the cultural changes needed in their own day-to-day practice. It was gratifying that the CPD activities which came to dominate the second phase of *Effective Practices in CPD* projects were those that incorporated the aspects which offered the greatest potential for impact in the classroom and across the school.

Our work with *Effective Practices in CPD* projects thus helped the schools involved to apply the key findings about successful practice to their own structures and processes. At the end of phase 1 we identified nine CPD approaches that had supported the most successful projects and were determining factors in professional development activity having an impact on colleagues' thinking and practice, the learning of pupils and organisational improvement. As noted in Chapter 1 these were:

- establishing clarity of purpose at the outset in CPD activity

- specifying a focus and goal for CPD activity, aligned to clear timescales
- including a focus on pupil outcomes in CPD activity
- ensuring participants' ownership of CPD activity
- engaging with a variety of CPD opportunities
- including time for reflection and feedback
- ensuring collaborative approaches to CPD
- developing strategic leadership of CPD
- understanding how to evaluate the impact of CPD.

We can re-order these approaches and select, first, those which particularly reflect the EPPI Centre research syntheses and which underpinned successful projects according to the project leaders:

- ensuring participants' ownership of CPD activity
- engaging with a variety of CPD opportunities
- including time for reflection and feedback
- ensuring collaborative approaches to CPD.

There was widespread agreement among project leaders that the above aspects had contributed greatly to the positive feelings of project participants and, indeed, motivated more colleagues to become involved, particularly support staff. This was shown very clearly in the special school reported on in Chapter 7.

Our experiences in the *Effective Practices in CPD* project then extended the EPPI findings. It was clear that

- including a focus on pupil outcomes in CPD activity

had stretched participants' thinking and had helped them to improve. This was the second highest rated approach that phase 2 project leaders selected through which to develop the effectiveness of their CPD practice following phase 1. The projects that tried to focus on pupil outcomes were also possibly able to be more detailed and clear in articulating their aims than others. For many of the project participants, linking CPD activity to desired pupil outcomes was not yet a natural or expected practice. The more usual link was between CPD activity and what colleagues would know or learn as a result. Phase 2 projects learned the value of identifying the desired change and improvement to pupil outcomes and then determining the nature of the CPD activity that would have the greatest effect in achieving such improvement: this is particularly explored in Chapter 8 with reference to Mathematics in the primary school.

It was also clear that the following aspects had supported the most successful projects:

- establishing clarity of purpose at the outset in CPD activity
- specifying a focus and goal for CPD activity, aligned to clear timescales.

To many project leaders, these two aspects represented a new way of thinking about CPD activity and were a significant challenge to their usual practices. They initially found it difficult to:

- be clear about what they wanted to improve *before* engaging in CPD activity
- be clear as to what was possible in a specified time frame
- identify the appropriate CPD activity to improve their starting point and so change and improve practice.

Consequently, they therefore struggled with evaluating whether they had achieved their intended outcome through engaging with CPD activity. To achieve this powerful link, described by Ofsted (2006) as a 'logical chain', we suggest that achieving clarity of purpose for CPD activity at the outset needs to be better understood as key to effective CPD.

The increasing sharpness of focus over the project's two phases demonstrated in the case studies indicates that clarity of outcomes supports the achievement of specific and demonstrable outcomes. This approach is a determining factor in the success highlighted in Chapter 5.

This leaves us with the following two approaches:

- developing strategic leadership of CPD
- understanding how to evaluate the impact of CPD.

Many of the project leaders did not necessarily have responsibility for CPD within their organisations: their learning about what constitutes effective CPD practice suggests that there is a great deal of scope to embed such understanding within middle and senior leaders in schools, including headteachers. Even when project leaders did have the lead role for CPD, it was clear that the role had not always been seen as having strategic significance. The ability to lead strategically in terms of professional development is linked to having clarity of purpose, identifying a clear goal (such as a focus on pupil outcomes) and being able to align this goal to a timescale for achievement. It is also about being able to evaluate the impact of CPD to celebrate success and so determine the next steps. The experience of the project leader in Chapter 5 helps here. She learned that the purpose of evaluating impact was to 'improve CPD activity'. It was not an end in itself. Impact evaluation is thus both the last link in a 'logical chain' and also the first.

The main lesson learned from the Effective Practices in CPD project is that for CPD activity to be effective, it needs to be underpinned by the nine CPD *approaches* identified earlier, irrespective of the CPD *activity*, the participants, the context or the setting. This means that any CPD activity (attending a course, observing work practice, joint planning or being coached, etc.) would be more effective and have a greater impact if these nine approaches underpinned all of the CPD activity in the organisation.

Professional development strategy and guidance over the last few years has encouraged schools to adopt CPD activities that have reflection, peer support and collaboration built into their DNA: this would include coaching and mentoring, networking and enquiry-based approaches. This has also meant an increasing focus on sharing internal expertise and a consequent reduction in the more traditional attendance at courses and conferences. However, this shift still means that CPD is seen as 'activities to be engaged in', albeit with some activities being more effective than others.

We would now suggest we need a further step change to ensure that CPD has the effect of supporting and influencing improvement for colleagues, for pupils and for organisations. As noted in the introduction, for CPD to be effective and so bring about improvement, it needs to be seen in terms of the consequent development of knowledge and expertise, which may (or may not) result from participating in a wide range of activities. The goal is the change effected in the thinking and practice of our colleagues so that such change improves the experience and learning for pupils. Of the three words within continuing professional development, we need a stronger focus on the *development* that comes from engaging in CPD activity: this complements the quality of the activity. To achieve this, the nine approaches that supported the most successful effective practice projects, and which are explored in the case studies, need to be better understood by schools and their CPD leaders as strategic ways in which the quality of any CPD activity and its subsequent impact can be improved.

The case studies presented in Part 2 highlight the levers and barriers to applying and implementing the nine CPD approaches within school structures and processes. Several strategies led to cultural shifts and success and were of value to all involved in the leadership of CPD.

Use of time

Innovation around the use of time for professional development activities is a constant theme. Time was used for staff to reflect individually and with each other about the effective implementation of new practices. A particularly effective example in Chapter 9 was organising extra non-contact time for early professional development (EPD) teachers and for support staff. The effect was different for both groups of staff. For support colleagues, 'just being together was powerful': it is often forgotten that support staff cannot always stay after school, and matching opportunities to the specific time needs of this group of staff paid real dividends. It helped to raise the status of support staff, with some learning mentors leading twilight sessions for other staff, including teachers, in understanding anger. For teachers in their second year, dedicated time for them to meet together to share experiences and solutions also enabled the school to develop more effective retention processes.

In other examples of more effective use of time, visiting and hosting visits from others to share good practice across schools, as in the local authority in Chapter 11, had a significant impact upon participants. A structured model of enquiry led to schools implementing change as a result of the conclusions of the enquiries and also from the learning of the enquiry teams.

> *We have been given the confidence to draw on the wealth of our own expertise...*

Coaching

Three case studies (Chapters 5–7) explored coaching as a CPD activity to improve practice. The examples reflected parallel developments. They began with a small number of interested people learning how to coach to deploying these skills and progressed to building a coaching culture and a more sustainable whole-school approach. The main lesson learned was that coaching was effective CPD practice when it supported and stimulated specific outcomes for colleagues and pupils rather than simply when a specific number of people had learned to coach.

In all cases, what is of interest is the way coaching supported, or was adopted, following engagement with other CPD activity. In particular, the combination of CPD activity, such as peer observations and coaching, had a very positive impact both as an effective strategy for improvement but also as a high-quality tool for change. Interestingly, this approach seemed to be supportive of teachers, middle leaders and support staff.

In the examples given, coaching helped to build a positive organisational culture through peer support and teamwork as well as further strengthening distributed leadership. The advantages were seen throughout the outcomes achieved: more coherent induction support led to improved team relationships; literacy practices and skills improved; teachers and support staff were better able to support the social and emotional development of pupils. Overall, relationships were enhanced, staff were more emotionally intelligent and appreciated the benefit of coaching and influencing over dogmatic telling. This led to greater motivation and higher staff morale.

Embedding learning to achieve change

The structure of the two phases of the *Effective Practices in CPD* project lent itself to a valuable lesson. The case studies that were able to embed and consolidate learning from the first phase of the project were more successful in bringing about sustained change and in being able to evaluate the impact of the strategies used to achieve such change. Many were able to draw on strategies that had worked before, such as using a small team of champions to help others to develop and implement change. In the instances where case study schools introduced a new focus at the beginning of phase 2, the success of the emerging work of phase 1 appeared diluted. This lesson has significant implications for the timescale needed to bring about embedded and sustained change as an outcome of professional development.

In Chapter 10, the project leaders found it difficult to identify any real impact across the school by the end of phase 1 and realised they needed to 'progress to greater knowledge and better practice'. Engaging in phase 2 (and so over a period of at least 15 months) enabled them to test out an idea for DIY CPD that a representative working party had created. In phase 2 they developed a whole-school approach to embed and consolidate the learning of phase 1 through the use of self-evaluation tools based on the National Standards for teachers and TAs to support professional reflection and further develop practice. Understanding the stages and time needed to bring about real learning and to embed this learning to support change is crucial to effective CPD. Professional development initiatives can flounder without working out the stages needed to improve and ensure consistency in the practice of all colleagues so that all pupils benefit.

This process is also powerful, even within a short period of time. In Chapter 5, change in the classroom practice of individual teachers was achieved within the short timescale of a coaching trios cycle as

> this gave urgency to the process, gave a specific focus and goal and spurred participants to achieve small-scale success.

Clarity as to intended impact within a specified timescale thus supports not only short-term and individual goals as above, it is essential to embedding change and success on a whole-school level.

Identifying and building on the progress made through effective CPD enabled teams, rather than just team leaders, to consolidate and embed changed practice.

> Staff engagement and involvement in the project was high with all teaching staff being involved to some degree. Most TAs led at least one lesson over the period of the project, with a particular focus on Maths.
>
> (Chapter 10)

> *The project's focus on all adults working together to develop one area of the children's learning rather than sending individuals on courses, meant that everyone was trialling similar ideas and techniques.*
>
> (Chapter 8)

Another key factor in consolidating changed practice was to embed the impact of the work of a small group of people into priorities identified in school development plans and self-evaluation forms (SEFs).

It is also true that the case study projects wished to build further on the progress already made. They are not finished and plan to embed and consolidate by formalising processes, with many intending to expand to involve more staff or other schools or to extend the professional learning to other environments, locations and contexts. A real learning culture has been created based on continual and sustained improvement. This is described very well in Chapter 11:

> *We have used the maxim that 'learning is the work' consciously and explicitly throughout the design of the project.*

This makes a powerful case for continuing professional development as being effective when it becomes embedded in the day-to-day practices of a school.

Impact evaluation

It has been argued that CPD is only effective when it makes a tangible difference to the attitudes, thinking and practice of colleagues and has the potential to make a difference for the organisation and for pupils. The key question is therefore how you can ascertain the difference CPD has made and the ways in which it has brought about improvement. The introductory chapter highlighted evidence which indicates that schools struggle with this aspect and this is clear in all of the case studies. Many made significant progress over the course of their projects, especially in understanding that impact evaluation is not an end in itself but a way to improve the quality of the intended outcomes. Project leaders were able to make greater use of a variety of methods to gather impact data, to identify what they were learning from that evidence and demonstrate greater clarity about the improvements they wanted to achieve.

Two particular aspects are worth spending time on to further our practice in this aspect:

- establishing baseline and impact pictures with supportive evidence
- understanding evidence sources and asserted or substantiated evidence.

Establishing baseline and impact pictures with supportive evidence

Taking the time to be clear about current practice and pupil learning (baseline) and the impact on practice and learning that you want to achieve within a desired timescale *before* engaging in sustained CPD activity is, we believe, crucial to evaluating impact. The most significant benefit to such clarity is to enable an effective match between the need for improvement and the type of CPD activity that will best effect such change.

This can be exemplified through the coaching case studies. An initial decision to develop a group of coaches can have an impact through sharing improved skills in colleagues. Developing coaches because this will improve the relationships between groups of staff and pupils opens the possibility of a link between CPD activity and pupil outcomes. The starting point (baseline) would, in this case, be strained relationships between staff and pupils, and a picture of the ways in which improved relationships would support the emotional and social development of pupils can then be painted. It is at this point that the most appropriate CPD activity – coaching – can be selected.

Chapter 6 gives an example of how this can be applied (see Table 12.2).

Table 12.2

	Before coaching	**After coaching**
Impact on performance of pupils	Pupils were writing in paragraphs which linked sentences on the same topics, but with little overall structure or use of signposting.	Focus on openings and connectives has helped pupils to produce more rounded paragraphs.

Chapter 11 offers a further example of this. A focus on pupil outcomes was implicit throughout this project with improvements to pupil learning expected to result from the findings of the enquiry walks. Enhancing pupil learning was always a core aim for the headteachers who felt that this project was about enabling and equipping them to do so more effectively. However, it was difficult for the participants to evaluate the specific impact of the enquiry walks on pupil outcomes: the latter needed to be made more explicit in the project design from the outset for participants to be able to capture evidence as the project progressed and at the end of the project. The next stage for this project would be to identify the intended gains in pupil learning to which the specific leadership and learning behaviours gained in this project would now lead.

This is a simple concept, yet the implications for CPD practice are far-reaching. This approach requires greater levels of understanding of the intended purpose of CPD activity for both individual colleagues and their team leaders. It requires higher levels of professional dialogue, especially in the performance management process, before the most effective CPD activity can be determined. Another hurdle is that the purpose of professional development tends to be explicit only in terms of the needs of adults. It is rare that improvements to the learning of pupils are articulated at the outset as the true purpose of CPD. If this link is made, it tends to be only at the level of a whole-school attainment target expressed in terms of levels or sublevels to be achieved. The development of individuals and teams brings about improvement in the learning of separate groups of pupils in separate classrooms at first, and it is at this level that we need to seek to impact upon pupils' learning. Only then can such improvements be aggregated to the whole-school level.

Understanding evidence sources and asserted or substantiated evidence

This aspect caused the greatest confusion for the case study participants. In the majority of cases the evidence cited for both the baseline picture and impact achieved was the source of the evidence only. This included line management meetings, lesson observations, interviews with staff, coaching conversations and reports from external coaches. It was rare for actual evidence to be offered from these sources as to what, for example, *'inconsistencies in practice'* actually were, what *'more collaboratively'* looked and sounded like in changed practice or what the *'effective systems and processes'* were – for either the practitioner or the pupils. In Chapter 4, for example, we are offered the u*se of questionnaires to ascertain what pupils like about the club.*

What is really interesting is what the pupils actually liked – what does the analysis of the questionnaires tell us? This then offers either a baseline from which to improve practice or a repeated questionnaire to indicate changed levels of satisfaction.

The need to investigate the evidence source and interrogate the evidence to interpret what it tells us about impact was especially marked when impact on adult practice or pupils' learning was cited. In the majority of cases, this evidence was asserted:

- The outcomes for teachers included improvements in planning and pedagogy – *such as?*
- Incremental improvement in reading ages – *from what to what?*
- Teaching and learning in this school had clearly improved overall, as seen by more personalised learning and improvements in the questioning skills of teachers – *such as ?*
- The speaking module for GCSE shows improved results – *from what to what?*

- The quality of teaching in the Sixth form improved – *from what to what?*

Project leaders were mostly reliant on asserting gains they had achieved at the conclusion of their project and found it difficult to use qualitative and quantitative data to substantiate such gains. It is surprising that schools are awash with data, yet the case study schools shied away from highlighting the precise data which would have highlighted links between the CPD activity and improved outcomes for colleagues and pupils. Why is this?

It was clear that schools felt the evidence was available and they were proud of their achievements, yet they had not seen the value of offering this to our case study researchers and the data were often inaccessible except by, for example, further mining of the spreadsheets. Schools seemed reluctant to do this, despite the fact that there is immense value in being able to celebrate the impact of professional development on specified improvements to colleagues' practice and substantiated improvements in the quality of learning as well as attainment.

In 'Motivating with Maths' (Chapter 8), data were offered as evidence of CPD activity leading to improved attainment.

There was a marked improvement in terms of children's achievement in Maths at all three key stages:

- *10 per cent increase in pupils achieving level 4 or above in the KS2 SATS*
- *24 per cent increase in pupils achieving level 2 or above in KS1 SATS*
- *23 per cent increase in pupils achieving six points or more in the aspect of Calculations in the Foundation Stage Profiles.*

This was a very helpful step forward and the participants were rightly proud of these achievements: this is something to celebrate. To build on this achievement we would suggest the information can be further supported by referencing the particular baseline and the period of time over which improvement was achieved. In terms of the baseline, are the figures given based on last year's cohort or the prior attainment of the particular pupils involved in the project? The difference is important, as it highlights the starting point for the improved attainment of the pupils. It is also valuable to reference the timescale so the size of the accomplishment is also noted.

A key lesson to learn then is why schools shy away from using the data they have gathered to highlight successful outcomes to CPD activity. One reason may be that the type of baseline data has not been identified or then gathered and it is then difficult to capture interim and final data, as there is a lack of clarity as to what the impact will look like. Possibly the language involved in capturing and analysing data for impact evaluation also gets in the way. Terms such as 'qualitative' or 'quantitative' evidence can be off-putting and is why alternatives such as 'hard' (numbers) and 'soft' (attitudes, perceptions, feelings, images, words) may be more useful. In all cases we would suggest it is important for the evidence to be substantiated rather than asserted.

A third reason why schools eschew existing data may be that they are not yet experienced enough in seeing the link between CPD activity and improvements in practice and pupils' learning. This can be explained by the current focus in most schools on the range and quality of CPD activity rather than a balanced focus on both quality of provision and impact on practice. If we wish professional development to change and improve practice in the classroom, and thus pupils' learning and experience, we also need a strong focus on evaluating impact through the concepts outlined here. This is important to motivate and value colleagues.

This would indicate that further development is needed in supporting schools and CPD leaders to interpret and analyse what the evidence source highlights in terms of changes to practice and learning to be achieved through engaging in CPD. This would offer a coherent understanding of the current situation and practice at the beginning of the proposed development, an improved ability to select appropriate evidence and increasing efforts to interpret and analyse this evidence. Case study projects found it hard to use *actual* qualitative or quantitative evidence from these sources to illustrate and substantiate their starting position. This ability is crucial in being able to identify appropriate CPD activity to bring about the consequent change and improvement, and then to evaluate the impact of such CPD activity. We recommend further work should continue in this respect: in particular, schools would benefit from seeing data used positively to determine a subsequent course of action and to demonstrate success and achievement.

What is clear is that all the case study schools worked hard to evaluate the impact of their improved CPD practice and that they were much more successful in this in phase 2 than in phase 1. It would be valuable to follow up the case study schools in subsequent years to see where their new-found skills take them.

Ways forward

The experiences of the case study schools show how significant the *Effective Practices in CPD* project has been. They highlight the real change in CPD thinking, practice and culture which has been achieved through involving schools and other organisations in testing, trialling, exploring and evaluating approaches to CPD. The case studies also document the lessons they have learned. These lessons are valuable for all schools and other support organisations in moving CPD practice forward.

The TDA's *Professional Development Strategy for the Children's Workforce in Schools (2009–12)*, launched in 2009, is important in ensuring that workforce development continues to be high on everyone's agenda. This is now a strategy for supporting all members of the school's workforce as opposed to looking at the development of teachers and other adults separately. The case study schools can be seen to have explored interesting and effective ways to involve and support all colleagues.

The TDA's strategy has three priorities. It wishes to:

- embed a learning culture
- increase coherence and collaboration
- improve quality and capacity.

The case study schools explored their own answers to addressing these strategic priorities and their experiences can support those of other schools and organisations in determining how to meet all three. Initiatives such as the *Effective Practices in CPD* project enable schools and their partners to develop, test out and implement CPD activities and approaches so that practitioners bring about cultural and strategic change and influence the development of national strategy.

To move forward and to meet the many challenges of professional development in twenty-first-century schools, we conclude with the following *recommendations*.

1. Schools and LAs would benefit from support to explore the strategic implications of the nine CPD approaches identified through the *Effective Practices in CPD* project.
2. Within these nine approaches, further support is needed to understand how to evaluate impact, especially as this is now an aspect of the Ofsted inspection schedule from September 2009. More significantly, there is a need to understand that evaluating impact is a learning tool that improves the quality of both the CPD activity and the outcomes achieved.
3. Schools and local authorities would benefit from further support to see the strategic value of establishing clarity of purpose at the outset of CPD engagement. This ability is crucial in being able to identify appropriate CPD activity to bring about the consequent change and improvement and to then evaluate the impact of such CPD activity.
4. Further development is also needed to enable educational organisations to interpret and analyse what evidence sources highlight in terms of achieving changes to practice and learning through engaging in CPD. Educational organisations would benefit from

seeing data used positively to determine a subsequent course of CPD activity and to demonstrate success and achievement.

The most valuable lesson learned from the *Effective Practices in CPD* case study schools is that the strategic implications of the nine CPD approaches identified can improve the overall quality and impact of professional development and so improve the learning for all children and young people. We look forward to being involved in supporting such improvement.

Footnote

1 Cordingley, P., Bell, M., Rundell, B. and Evans, D. (2003) *The Impact of Collaborative CPD on Classroom Teaching and Learning*. Research Evidence in Education Library. London: EPPI Centre, Social Science Research Unit, Institute of Education, University of London.

Cordingley, P., Bell, M., Evans, D. and Firth, A. (2005) *The Impact of Collaborative CPD on Classroom Teaching and Learning. Review: What do teacher impact data tell us about collaborative CPD?* Research Evidence in Education Library. London: EPPI Centre, Social Science Research Unit, Institute of Education, University of London.

Cordingley, P., Bell, M., Thomason, S. and Firth, A. (2005) *The Impact of Collaborative Continuing Professional Development (CPD) on Classroom Teaching and Learning. Review: How do collaborative and sustained CPD and sustained but not collaborative CPD affect teaching and learning?* Research Evidence in Education Library. London: EPPI Centre, Social Science Research Unit, Institute of Education, University of London.

Cordingley P., Bell, M., Isham, C., Evans, D. and Firth, A. (2007) *What do Specialists do in CPD Programmes for which there is Evidence of Positive Outcomes for Pupils and Teachers? Report.* Research Evidence in Education Library. London: EPPI Centre, Social Science Research Unit, Institute of Education, University of London.

References

Bubb, S. and Earley, P. (2010) *Helping Staff Develop in Schools.* London: Sage.

Bubb, S. and Earley, P. (2007) *Leading and Managing Continuing Professional Development* (second edition). London: Sage.

Cordingley, P., Bell, M., Rundell, B. and Evans, D. (2003) *The Impact of Collaborative CPD on Classroom Teaching and Learning.* Research Evidence in Education Library. London: EPPI Centre, Social Science Research Unit, Institute of Education, University of London.

Cordingley, P., Bell, M., Evans, D. and Firth, A. (2005) *The Impact of Collaborative CPD on Classroom Teaching and Learning. Review: What do teacher impact data tell us about collaborative CPD?* Research Evidence in Education Library. London: EPPI Centre, Social Science Research Unit, Institute of Education, University of London.

Cordingley, P., Bell, M., Thomason, S. and Firth, A. (2005) *The Impact of Collaborative Continuing Professional Development (CPD) on Classroom Teaching and Learning. Review: How do collaborative and sustained CPD and sustained but not collaborative CPD affect teaching and learning?* Research Evidence in Education Library. London: EPPI Centre, Social Science Research Unit, Institute of Education, University of London.

Cordingley, P., Bell, M., Isham, C., Evans, D. and Firth, A. (2007) *What do Specialists do in CPD Programmes for which there is Evidence of Positive Outcomes for Pupils and Teachers? Report.* Research Evidence in Education Library. London: EPPI Centre, Social Science Research Unit, Institute of Education, University of London.

Frost, D. and Durrant, J. (2003) *Teacher-led Development Work.* London: David Fulton.

Goodall, J., Day, C., Harris, A., Lindsey, G. and Muijs, D. (2005) *Evaluating the Impact of Continuing Professional Development.* Nottingham: DCSF. Available at: http://dcsf.gov.uk/rsgateway

Guskey, T. (2000) *Evaluating Professional Development*. New York: Corwin.

Ofsted (2006) *The Logical Chain*. London: Ofsted.

Porritt, V. (2005) *London's Learning: Developing the Leadership of CPD*. London: Department for Education and Skills.

Porritt, V. (2009) 'Evaluating the impact of professional development'. *Education Journal,* Issue 116.

Porritt, V., Episcopo, K. and Wybron, S. (2006) 'London's learning: developing the leadership of CPD in London schools'. *Professional Development Today*, Volume 9, Issue 1.

Training and Development Agency for Schools (2006) *The Impact of Postgraduate Professional Development (PPD) Courses*. London: TDA.

Training and Development Agency for Schools (2007) *Impact Evaluation of CPD*. Available at: http://www.tda.gov.uk/upload/resources/pdf/i/impact_evaluation. pdf

Training and Development Agency for Schools (2008) *Continuing Professional Development Guidance (CPD)*. London: TDA.